CONTRACT FORMS
FOR
REAL ESTATE AND LEASES
Robert Ogden Cottrell

Ogden Shepard Publishing Company
Boulder, Colorado   80302

WRITE YOUR OWN CONTRACTS workbooks are designed to facilitate the public's understanding and use of contracts. However, the sample contracts herein are not meant to replace legal counsel. You should be further advised that laws, local requirements, and customary practices vary from state to state or from jurisdiction to jurisdiction and you are therefore encouraged to always consult an attorney when undertaking any legal action. The author and publisher are not engaged in providing legal services and are not responsible or liable for any loss or damages whatsoever, including all direct and consequential damages, which may be incurred as a result of the use of these sample contracts or the manner in which they are used.

Copyright © 1986 By:
Ogden Shepard Publishing Co., Inc.
2305 Canyon Blvd. #205
Boulder, CO   80302
303-444-2303

Write Your Own Contracts Series
ISBN 0-937313-03-3

Write Your Own Contracts — Real Estate And Leases
ISBN 0-937313-33-5

Published by Ogden Shepard Publishing Company

Printed in the United States of America

CONTENTS

CONTENTS, continued

INTRODUCTION

WRITE YOUR OWN CONTRACTS workbooks contain examples of the contracts most commonly used in the United States today. The purpose of the series is NOT to replace attorneys. The purpose is to take some of the mystery and expense from contractual work by making these practice contract forms accessible to the general public.

Each workbook in the series has a wide range of sample contract forms pertaining to the area designated by the workbook's title. These forms are simplified in layout and language to make them easy to read and understand. Additionally, each workbook has a glossary defining the terms found in the contracts of that particular workbook.

Many forms found in **WRITE YOUR OWN CONTRACTS** are so uncomplicated they can be taken from the workbooks and used right away. There will be times, of course, when readers will decide to get some legal help. In these cases, the readers who already have gathered pertinent information and familiarized themselves with contractual demands will be able to realize a substantial savings in their legal expenses.

HOW TO USE **WRITE YOUR OWN CONTRACTS**

WRITE YOUR OWN CONTRACTS workbooks are designed to be easy to use. The Table of Contents lists the sample contract forms contained in a particular workbook. When you locate the sample contract form applicable to your needs, you may want to make photocopies of it or remove the form from the workbook.

If you choose to keep **WRITE YOUR OWN CONTRACTS** intact, it's easy to make copies of the pages you need. Most copy machines have a platen or a cover which can be raised to accommodate books and magazines. Simply hold the pages to be copied flat against the glass plate to get an accurate print. It is possible that you will have to "break" the book's binding so the entire page can lie flat.

If you wish to remove a sample contract from the book, use a razor blade, sharp knife or scissors to cut along the black dashes which run vertically at the book's binding.

If you are going to use a typewriter when filling out the practice contract forms, our samples are set up to use a 12-pitch (12 characters to an inch) format.

GLOSSARY OF TERMS

ABANDONMENT   To give up rights, property or a family relationship by desertion, with no intention to return or reclaim.

ABSTRACT OF TITLE   A chronological summary of the successful titles (evidence of ownership) to a piece of real estate.

ACCEPTANCE   The creating of a binding contract by receiving something with the intention of keeping it. Also, creating a binding contract by agreeing to the terms of an offer.

ACKNOWLEDGMENT   When a NOTARY PUBLIC notarizes a document. Some state jurisdictions require an acknowledgment for each party signing certain types of contracts.

ACT OF GOD   In insurance and law, an inevitable, accidental or extraordinary event which cannot be foreseen and guarded against, such as lightning, tornados, earthquakes, etc.

ADDENDUM   Something added; a supplement.

AFFIDAVIT   A written and signed statement sworn to under oath.

APPURTENANCE   The buildings, rights and improvements which belong to a house or land. This includes outbuildings, pastures and gardens to a house, and a right of way and other easements to land. Land can never properly pass as an appurtenance to land.

APPURTENANT   Belonging to or annexed; pertaining to a right; such as a right of way appurtenant to land.

ASSIGN   To convey or transfer to another, as to assign property, rights or interests to another.

ASSUMABLE MORTGAGE   Purchaser takes ownership of real estate encumbered by an existing mortgage and assumes responsibility as the guarantor for the unpaid balance of the mortgage.

ATTORNEY-IN-FACT   A person, not necessarily an attorney, who has a written and signed POWER OF ATTORNEY to transact business and act on behalf of another person.

BALLOON PAYMENT   A final payment that is more than twice the amount of the earlier, regular payments.

BANKRUPT   The condition of an insolvent debtor in which his or her property is turned over, under jurisdiction of a federal bankruptcy court, to a trustee to be distributed for the benefit of creditors.

BINDING   Causing to be bound from a legal or moral standpoint.

BREACH   An intentional or unintentional infraction of the law, a failure to fulfill an obligation or breaking one's written or oral contract or promise.

CARRY-BACK FINANCING   When the purchaser requests owner financing of a new first or second deed of trust (or a third, etc.).

GLOSSARY

CHATTEL   An article of personal or movable property as distinguished from real property.

CHOSE IN ACTION   A thing that is recoverable in a law suit.

CLEAR TITLE   A title to property that has been determined to be free from all liens and encumbrances.

CLOUD ON A TITLE   A defect in a title to property that could diminish the rights of the owners.

CONDEMNATION   A legal declaration taking privately-owned real estate for public use without the owner's consent but with payment of compensation. It may be done in accordance with the government's right of EMINANT DOMAIN. Also, declaring premises to be unsafe for habitation.

CONSIDERATION   The price or inducement of a contract; necessary for a contract to be binding.

CONTRACT   A legally enforceable, explicit, written agreement between two or more parties and made for a consideration.

CONVENTIONAL MORTGAGE   A loan that is neither insured by the Federal Housing Administration nor guaranteed by the Veterans Administration.

COTENANCY   A tenancy by several distinct titles but by unity of possession, or any joint ownership or common interest with its grantor. The term is broad enough to comprise both tenancy in common and joint tenancy.

COVENANT   An agreement or special provision of a deed or a lease fixing certain uses and nonuses of property or promising certain things to be done or not be done by landlord or tenant. A real covenant in a deed is binding on future owners of land. A restrictive covenant is an agreement written into a deed or lease prohibiting certain uses or disposal of land. To covenant is to promise by means of a covenant.

DEED   A document under seal used to transfer ownership of real property.

DEFAULT   Failure to meet a legal obligation as in failure to pay a debt when it is due. Also, failure to take steps required in a legal action.

DEMISED PREMISES   Leased premises.

DISCLAIMER   In law, an express or implied denial or renunciation of certain things in question.

EARNEST MONEY   The deposit made by a buyer on a purchase that binds the buyer and purchaser to the terms of the sales agreement. In a LIQUIDATED DAMAGES contract the earnest money is the seller's only recourse if the purchaser is in default.

EASEMENT   The legal right to use a limited portion of another's land for a specific purpose such as right of way, access to water, air, etc., or a user's access to his or her own land.

GLOSSARY

EMINENT DOMAIN   The power of government over all property within its limits by which it can take property for public use without owner's consent by giving just compensation to owner.

ENCROACHMENT   Intruding or trespassing on another's property or rights.

ENCUMBRANCE   A lien or claim against real or personal property.

ENDORSER   One who signs his or her name on a legal document, as to endorse a check upon cashing or to endorse (cosign) the note of another to guarantee payment in the event the original signer defaults.

EQUITY   The difference between the fair market value of property and the homeowner's indebtedness (MORTGAGE).

ESCROW   A written agreement, as a bond or deed, delivered to a third party to be held until some certain conditions of an agreement between other parties have been met.

ESCROW PAYMENT   That portion of a mortgagor's monthly payment held in trust by the lender to pay for taxes, hazard insurance, lease payments, and other items as they become due. In some states, called impounds.

EXCHANGE   The trading of an equity in a piece of property for the equity in another.

EXHIBIT   A paper or document produced and exhibited to a court during a trial, hearing or to a commission taking depositions, or to auditors, arbitrators, and so on as a voucher or proof of facts or as otherwise connected with the subject matter. The exhibit, in being accepted, is marked for identification and annexed to the deposition, report or other principal document or is filed on record or otherwise made part of the case.

FHA LOAN   A type of mortgage loan funded by saving and loan associations, commercial banks and mortgage loan brokers that is insured by the Federal Housing Administration.

GOOD TITLE   A title of ownership to real or personal property that is free from valid liens, claims and encumbrances, making it a valid and marketable title.

HIRES   Leases.

HOLDOVER TENANT   A tenant who keeps possession of property past the expiration date of his or her lease.

INDEMNIFY   To protect against or keep free from loss, damage, etc.; to insure. To redeem or make good a loss.

INTEREST   Money paid for use of money; the rate of such payment.

JOINT TENANCY   The joint ownership of real property by two or more persons with the right of survivorship.

GLOSSARY

JURAT In law, a statement added to an affidavit, telling when and before whom the affidavit was made.

LANDLORD The owner of real property who rents or leases it to another.

LESSEE One who leases or rents property. The owner of the property is called the landlord or the lessor.

LEVY To impose or assess a tax.

LIEN A legal claim one person has against the property of another as security for a debt.

LIQUIDATED DAMAGES A certain sum of money, which was agreed upon by the parties to a contract, to be paid by one to the other in event of a default or breach of the contract.

MAKER One who makes or signs a promissory note payable to another.

MARKETABLE TITLE A title that any reasonably-informed buyer can assume to be sufficiently free and clear of encumbrances for the transaction of business.

MERCHANTABLE That which can be marketed.

MORTGAGE/DEED OF TRUST Pledge of real property to secure a debt by a written instrument given by the mortgagor. Should be recorded in the county recorder's office.

NOTARY PUBLIC A person authorized by law to perform certain public functions such as witnessing signatures, administrating oaths and taking affidavits. Most banks have notaries public whose services are either free or for a nominal rate.

NOTE A written promise to pay a certain amount of money.

PLAT A map of an area showing the streets, lots and boundary markers, including survey measurements.

POWER OF ATTORNEY A written document giving a person the legal authority to act in behalf of another to the degree specified in the document. A power of attorney concerning real property, which includes all general powers of attorney, should be notarized and be recorded at the county recorder's office where the property in question is located.

PREPAYMENT PENALTY A fee paid to a mortgagee when mortgagor pays the mortgage off before it becomes due. Also known as a prepayment fee or reinvestment fee.

PRIVATE MORTGAGE INSURANCE (PMI) Insurance written by a private company protecting the mortgage lender against loss occasioned by a mortgage default.

QUIET ENJOYMENT The tenant's right, implied or expressed by a covenant in a lease, not to be wrongfully disturbed by acts or omissions of the landlord or anyone claiming paramount title.

GLOSSARY

QUITCLAIM   To give up a claim.

QUITCLAIM DEED   A deed relinquishing all claims to property or right, but not guaranteeing against claims made by another.

QUIT THE PREMISES   To leave permanently with one's belongings.

REAL PROPERTY   Real estate; land, buildings and fixtures permanently attached to it.

RECITAL   The formal statement of setting forth of some matter of fact in order to explain the reasons upon which the transaction is founded.

REMEDY   The desired result of an action.

RIGHT OF FIRST REFUSAL   A temporary right for a designated period of time that one person has to purchase or lease property at a certain price, after a subsequent party has submitted an offer to lease or purchase from the owner.

RIGHT OF WAY   The right to pass over another person's land at a particular place.

SCHEDULE   A sheet of paper annexed to a statute, deed, deposition or other instrument, exhibiting in detail all matters mentioned or referred to in the principal document.

SEAL   To authenticate or confirm. A stamp or other device used to certify or authenticate a document.

SECURE   To make certain of payment, as by bond, surety, etc. To warrant or insure against loss.

SECURITY DEPOSIT   The money left with the landlord by a tenant to insure that the tenant will abide by the rules of the lease agreement. A landlord may use part or all of the security deposit to pay for any damages done by the tenant. Such a deposit may also be used to pay LIQUIDATED DAMAGES in the event that a tenant requests premature termination of the lease.

SHARED EQUITY (APPRECIATION) MORTGAGE   Mortgage where the lender shares in a portion of the appreciation of a property that occurs after the loan is made, usually at a specified time in the future or at time of sale.

SPECIFIC PERFORMANCE   The right of a party to a contract to enforce the terms of the contract against a party in default rather than just accept damages. It must be included as a remedy to that party in the terms of the contract to be enforced. Enforcement is through an action brought in district court.

SUBORDINATION   An agreement by a lender to place his or her mortgage or deed of trust behind a subsequent loan secured by the same property even though the subsequent loan is recorded later. The subsequent loan would receive priority of pay-off upon sale or foreclosure of the secured property.

GLOSSARY

TENANCY IN COMMON   Ownership of real property by two or more people, each with an undivided interest in it and all with equal right to possession of it. The undivided interests may or may not be equal. At death of a tenant in common, his or her interest does not pass on to the surviving owners but becomes part of his or her estate.

TENANT   One who holds title, lease, right to possession of real property.

TIME IS OF THE ESSENCE   Limitations after which neither party can demand an extension of performance.

TITLE   Legal ownership of property, often used interchangeably with the word "ownership"; a document proving ownership.

TITLE INSURANCE   An insurance policy which protects the insured (the purchaser or lender) against loss arising from defects in title.

VA LOAN   Loan available to certain veterans, that is funded by savings and loan associations, commercial banks and mortgage loan brokers and is guaranteed and administered by the Veterans Administration.

VALUABLE CONSIDERATION   Anything of value given in exchange for performance or the promise of performance by another.

VALUATIONS   Estimating value or worth, as the valuation of property.

WAIVER   A voluntary relinquishment or renunciation of a claim, a right or privilege.

WARRANTY   A statement of assurance by a seller or a manufacturer that goods are as represented to the buyer. Also, the assurance that goods or property will be repaired and made serviceable if found defective within a stipulated period of time.

WRAP AROUND MORTGAGE (ALL-INCLUSIVE DEED OF TRUST)   A second mortgage where an underlying deed of trust loan balance is included in the new mortgage. Purchaser buying under a wrap-around mortgage may either assume the underlying mortgage or purchase subject to the underlying mortgage. The interest rate applicable to the wrap-around mortgage need not be the same as that applicable to the underlying loan. Purchaser pays the interest rate applicable to the wrap-around mortgage on the entire mortgage amount of the underlying mortgage.

BILLS OF SALE

BILL OF SALE: REAL PROPERTY

Agreement made _____, 19____, between:
(month and day)   (yr)

_____   and   _____
(Name(s) of buyer(s))   (Name(s) of seller(s))

herein known as buyer, of   herein known as seller, of

_____   _____
(Address)   (Address)

_____   _____
(City)   (City)

_____   _____
(County)   (County)

_____   _____
(State)   (State)

KNOW ALL MEN BY THESE PRESENTS: That _____, for and
(name of seller)

in consideration of the sum of _____ Dollars ($_____)

to him in hand paid, at or before the ensealing or delivery of these presents by

_____, the receipt of which is hereby
(name of buyer)

acknowledged, has bargained and sold, and by these presents does grant and convey

unto the said buyer, his personal representatives, successors and assigns, the

following property, goods and chattels, to wit: _____

_____

_____

_____

_____

Page 1 of 3

BILL OF SALE: REAL PROPERTY - Continued

_____

_____

_____

_____

_____

_____

located at
```
                  _____
                  (Address)


                  _____
                  (City)


                  _____
                  (County)


                  _____
                  (State)
```

TO HAVE AND TO HOLD the same unto the said buyer, his personal representatives, successors and assigns, forever. The said seller covenants and agrees to and with the buyer, his personal representatives, successors and assigns, to WARRANT AND DEFEND the sale of said property, goods and chattels, against all and every person or persons whomever. When used herein, the singular shall include the plural, the plural the singular, and the use of any gender shall be applicable to all genders.

IN WITNESS WHEREOF: the parties hereto have set their hands and seals the day and year first written above.

_____   _____
(Signature of buyer)   (Signature of seller)

_____   _____
(Signature of buyer)   (Signature of seller)

Page 2 of 3

BILL OF SALE: REAL PROPERTY - Continued

STATE OF _____

City of _____)

)

County of _____)

I hereby certify that this instrument was filed for record in my office this

_____ day of _____, 19____, at

_____ o'clock _____.M., and is duly recorded in Book

_____, Page _____, Film No. _____ Reception

No. _____.

                                 _____
                                 (Recorder)

By   _____
                                 (Deputy)

                        Fee $_____

COMMERCIAL LEASES

LEASE OF BUSINESS PREMISES

Agreement made _____ , 19____ , between:
(month and day)   (yr)

_____ and _____
(Name(s) of tenant)   (Name(s) of landlord)

herein referred to as tenant, of   herein referred to as landlord, of

_____   _____
(Address)   (Address)

_____   _____
(City)   (City)

_____   _____
(County)   (County)

_____   _____
(State)   (State)

   In consideration of the mutual covenants contained herein, the parties agree as follows:

SECTION ONE - DESCRIPTION OF PREMISES - Landlord leases to tenant the premises located at
_____
(Address)

_____
(City)

_____
(County)

_____
(State)

and described more particularly as follows: _____
(insert legal description)

_____.

Page 1 of 10

LEASE OF BUSINESS PREMISES - Continued

SECTION TWO - TERM - The term of this lease is _____ years, beginning
                                                          (number)

on _____, 19 ___, and terminating on _____, 19 ___, at
     (month and day)   (yr)   (month and day)   (yr)

_____ o'clock ____.m.

SECTION THREE - RENT - The total rent under this lease is _____

Dollars ($_____). Tenant shall pay landlord that amount in installments of

_____ Dollars ($_____) each month, beginning on

_____, 19 ___, with succeeding payments due on the _____
 (month and day)   (yr)   (number)

day of each month thereafter during the term of the lease.

SECTION FOUR - USE OF PREMISES - The premises are to be used for the purposes of

_____.
(specify purpose)

Tenant shall restrict its use to such purposes, and shall not use or permit the

use of the premises for any other purpose without the written consent of landlord.

SECTION FIVE - RESTRICTIONS ON USE - Tenant shall not use the premises in any

manner that will increase risks covered by insurance on the premises and result in

an increase in the rate of insurance or a cancellation of any insurance policy,

even if such use may be in furtherance of tenant's business purposes. Tenant

shall not keep, use, or sell anything prohibited by any policy of fire insurance

covering the premises, and shall comply with all requirements of the insurers

applicable to the premises necessary to keep in force the fire-and-liability

insurance.

SECTION SIX - WASTE, NUISANCE, OR UNLAWFUL ACTIVITY - Tenant shall not allow any

waste or nuisance on the premises, or use or allow the premises to be used for any

unlawful purpose.

LEASE OF BUSINESS PREMISES - Continued

SECTION SEVEN - DELAY IN DELIVERING POSSESSION - This lease shall not be rendered void or voidable by the inability of landlord to deliver possession to tenant on the date set forth in SECTION TWO, and landlord shall not be liable to tenant for any loss or damage suffered by reason of such a delay; provided, however, that landlord does deliver possession no later than _____, 19 ____. In the
(month and day)   (yr)

event of a delay in delivering possession, the rent for the period of such delay will be deducted from the total rent due under the lease. No extension of the lease shall result from a delay in delivering possession.

SECTION EIGHT - UTILITES- Tenant shall be responsible for paying the following utilities or services connected with the premises (check those applicable):

_____	water	_____	phone
_____	sewer	_____	trash pick up
_____	electricity	_____	Other: _____
_____	gas	_____	Other: _____

SECTION NINE - REPAIRS AND MAINTENANCE - Tenant shall maintain the premises and keep them in good repair at tenant's expense, except the side and rear exterior walls and the roof which will be maintained in good condition by landlord. Tenant shall maintain and repair windows, doors, skylights, adjacent sidewalks, the building front, and interior walls.

SECTION TEN - DELIVERY, ACCEPTANCE, AND SURRENDER OF PREMISES - Landlord represents that the premises are in fit condition for use by tenant. Acceptance of the premises by tenant shall be construed as recognition that the premises are in good state of repair and in sanitary condition. Tenant shall surrender the

LEASE OF BUSINESS PREMISES - Continued

premises at the end of the lease term, or any renewal thereof, in the same condition as when tenant took possession, allowing for reasonable use and wear, and damage by acts of God, including fires and storms. Before delivery, tenant shall remove all business signs placed on the premises by tenant and restore the portion of the premises on which they were placed on the same condition as when received.

SECTION ELEVEN - PARTIAL DESTRUCTION OF PREMISES - Partial destruction of the leased premises shall not render this lease void or voidable, nor terminate it except as herein provided. If the premises are partially destroyed during the term of this lease, landlord shall repair them when such repairs can be made in conformity with governmental laws and regulations, within _____ days (number) of the partial destruction. Written notice of the intention of landlord to repair shall be given to tenant within _____ days after any partial (number) destruction. Rent will be reduced proportionately to the extent to which the repair operations interfer with the business conducted on the premises by tenant. If the repairs cannot be made within the time specified above, landlord shall have the option to make them within a reasonable time and continue this lease in effect with proportional rent rebate to tenant as provided for herein. If the repairs cannot be made in _____ days, and if landlord does not elect to make (number) them within a reasonable time, either party shall have the option to terminate this lease.

Disputes between landlord and tenant relating to provisions of this section shall be arbitrated. The parties shall each select an arbitrator, and the two arbitrators selected shall together select a third arbitrator. The three

LEASE OF BUSINESS PREMISES - Continued

arbitrators shall determine the dispute, and their decisions shall be binding on the parties. The parties shall divide the costs of arbitration equally between them.

SECTION TWELVE - ENTRY ON PREMISES BY LESSOR - Landlord reserves the right to enter on the premises at reasonable times to inspect them, perform required maintenance and repairs, or make additions, alterations, or modifications to any part of the building in which the premises are located, and tenant shall permit landlord to do so. Landlord may erect scaffolding, fences, and similar structures, post relevant notices, and place moveable equipment in connection with making alterations, additions, or repairs, all without incurring liability to tenant for disturbance of quiet enjoyment of the premises, or loss of occupation thereof.

SECTION THIRTEEN - SIGNS, AWNINGS, AND MARQUEES INSTALLED BY TENANT - Tenant shall not construct or place signs, awnings, marquees, or other structures projecting from the exterior of the premises without the written consent of landlord. Tenant shall remove signs, displays, advertisements, or decorations tenant has placed on the premises that, in the opinion of landlord, are offensive or otherwise objectionable. If tenant fails to remove such signs, displays, advertisements, or decorations within _____ days after receiving written notice from
(number)
landlord to remove them, landlord reserves the right to enter the premises and remove them at the expense of tenant.

SECTION FOURTEEN - BUSINESS SALE SIGNS - Tenant shall not conduct "Quitting Business," "Lost Our Lease," "Bankruptcy," or other sales of that nature on the premises without the written consent of landlord.

LEASE OF BUSINESS PREMISES - Continued

SECTION FIFTEEN - NONLIABILITY OF LANDLORD FOR DAMAGES - Landlord shall not be liable for liability or damage claims for injury to persons or property from any cause relating to the occupancy of the premises during the term of this lease or any extension thereof. Tenant shall indemnify landlord from all liability, loss, or other damage claims or obligations resulting from any injuries or losses of this nature.

SECTION SIXTEEN - LIABILITY INSURANCE - Tenant shall procure and maintain in force at tenant's expense during the term of this lease and any extension thereof public liability insurance with insurers and through brokers approved by landlord. Such coverage shall be adequate to protect against liability for damage claims through public use of or arising out of accidents occurring in or around the leased premises, in a minimum amount of _____ Dollars ($_____) for each person injured, _____ Dollars ($_____) for any one accident, and _____ Dollars ($_____) for property damage. The insurance policies shall provide coverage for contingent liability of landlord on any claims or losses. The policies shall be delivered to landlord for keeping. Tenant shall obtain a written obligation from the insurers to notify landlord in writing at least _____ days prior to cancellation
                                                              (number)
or refusal to renew any policy. If the insurance policies are not kept in force during the entire term of this lease or any extension thereof, landlord may procure the necessary insurance and pay the premium therefor, and the premium shall be repaid to landlord as an additional rent installment for the month following the date on which the premiums were paid by landlord.

SECTION SEVENTEEN - ASSIGNMENT, SUBLEASE, OR LICENSE - Tenant shall not assign or sublease the premises, or any right or privilege connected therewith, or allow any

LEASE OF BUSINESS PREMISES - Continued

other person except agents and employees of tenant to occupy the premises or any part thereof without first obtaining the written consent of landlord. A consent by landlord shall not be a consent to a subsequent assignment, sublease, or occupation by other persons. An unauthorized assignment, sublease, or license to occupy by tenant shall be void and shall terminate the lease at the option of landlord. The interest of tenant in this lease is not assignable by operation of law without the written consent of landlord.

SECTION EIGHTEEN - BREACH - The appointment of a receiver to take possession of the assets of tenant, a general assignment for the benefit of the creditors of tenant, any action taken or allowed to be taken by tenant under any bankruptcy act, or the failure of tenant to comply with each and every term and condition of this lease shall constitute a breach of this lease. Tenant shall have

_____ days after receipt of written notice from landlord of any breach
(number)

to correct the conditions specified in the notice, or if the corrections cannot be made within the _____-day period, tenant shall have a reasonable time to
(number)

correct the default if action is commenced by tenant within _____ days
(number)

after receipt of the notice.

SECTION NINETEEN - REMEDIES OF LANDLORD FOR BREACH BY TENANT - Landlord shall have the following remedies in addition to other rights and remedies in event tenant breaches this lease agreement and fails to make corrections as set forth in SECTION EIGHTEEN:

1. Landlord may re-enter the premises immediately and remove the property and personnel of tenant, store the property in a public warehouse or at a place selected by landlord, at the expense of tenant.

LEASE OF BUSINESS PREMISES - Continued

2. After re-entry landlord may terminate the lease on giving _____
                                                                (number)

    days' written notice of termination to tenant. Without such notice, re-entry

    will not terminate the lease. On termination landlord may recover from tenant

    all damages proximately resulting from the breach, including the cost of

    recovering the premises and the part of the balance of this lease over the

    reasonable rental value of the premises for the remainder of the lease term,

    which sum shall be immediately due landlord from tenant.

3. After re-entering, landlord may re-rent the premises or any part thereof for

    any term without terminating the lease, at such rent and on such terms as

    landlord may choose. Landlord may make alterations and repairs to the

    premises. The duties and liabilities of the parties if the premises are re-

    rented as provided herein shall be as follows:

    a) In addition to tenant's liability to landlord for breach of the lease,

        tenant shall be liable for all expenses of the re-renting, for the

        alterations and repairs made, and for the difference between the rent

        received by landlord under the new lease agreement and the rent

        installments that are due for the same period under this lease.

    b) Landlord at landlord's option shall have the right to apply the rent

        received from re-renting the premises (1) to reduce tenant's indebtedness

        to landlord under the lease, not including indebtedness for rent, (2) to

        expenses of the re-renting and alterations and repairs made, (3) to rent

        due under this lease, or (4) to payment of future rent under this lease as

        it becomes due.

    If the new tenant does not pay a rent installment promptly to landlord, and

    the rent installment has been credited in advance of payment to the

    indebtedness of tenant other than rent, or if rentals from the new tenant have

LEASE OF BUSINESS PREMISES - Continued

been otherwise applied by landlord as provided for herein, and during any rent installment period, are less than the rent payable for the corresponding installment period under this lease, tenant shall pay landlord the deficiency, separately for each rent installment deficiency period, and before the end of that period. Landlord may at any time after such re-renting terminate the lease for the breach on which landlord based the re-entry and re-rented the premises.

4. After re-entry, landlord may procure the appointment of a receiver to take possession and collect rents and profits of the business of tenant, and, if necessary, to collect the rents and profits the receiver may carry on the business of tenant and take possession of the personal property used in the business of tenant, including inventory, trade fixtures, and furnishings and use them in the business without compensating tenant. Proceedings for appointment of a receiver by landlord, or the appointment of a receiver and the conduct of the business of tenant by the receiver, shall not terminate and forfeit this lease unless landlord has given written notice of termination to tenant as provided herein.

SECTION TWENTY - ATTORNEYS' FEES - If landlord files an action to enforce any agreement contained in this lease, or for breach of any covenant or condition, tenant shall pay landlord reasonable attorneys' fees for any litigation, all fees to be fixed by the court.

SECTION TWENTY-ONE - CONDEMNATION - Eminent domain proceedings resulting in the condemnation of a part of the premises leased herein, but leaving the remaining premises usable by tenant for the purposes of business, will not terminate this lease unless landlord, at landlord's option, terminates the lease by giving written notice of termination to tenant. The effect of any condemnation, where

LEASE OF BUSINESS PREMISES - Continued

the option to terminate is not exercised, will be to terminate the lease as to the portion of the premises condemned, and the lease of the remainder of the demised premises shall remain intact. The rental for the remainder of the lease term shall be reduced by the amount that the usefulness of the premises has been reduced for the business purposes of tenant. Tenant hereby assigns and transfers to landlord any claim tenant may have to compensation for damages as a result of any condemnation.

SECTION TWENTY-TWO - OPTION TO RENEW - Landlord grants to tenant an option to renew this lease for _____
    (another term equal to the term hereof/as the case may be)
at a rental of _____ Dollars ($_____) per month, with all other terms and conditions of the renewal lease to be the same as those herein. To exercise this option to renew, tenant must give landlord written notice of intention to do so at least _____ days before this lease expires.
                               (number)

   In witness whereof, the parties have executed this lease in the City of _____, State of _____, the day and the year first above written.

_____   _____
(Signature of landlord)   (Signature of tenant)

_____   _____
(Signature of landlord)   (Signature of tenant)

If required by state law, two witnesses for landlord and two witnesses for tenant should sign this agreement:

_____   _____
(Witness for landlord)   (Witness for tenant)

_____   _____
(Witness for landlord)   (Witness for tenant)

LEASE OF OFFICE SPACE

Agreement made _____, 19____, between:
                     (month and day)   (yr)

_____   and   _____
(Name(s) of tenant)   (Name(s) of landlord)

herein referred to as tenant, of   herein referred to as landlord, of

_____   _____
(Address)   (Address)

_____   _____
(City)   (City)

_____   _____
(County)   (County)

_____   _____
(State)   (State)

RECITALS

1. Landlord is the sole owner of the business premises described below having office space therein to rent.

2. Tenant is in the business of _____
                                 (type of business)

   and desires to lease office space from landlord.

3. The parties desire to enter a lease agreement defining their respective rights, duties, and liabilities relating to the premises.

In consideration of the mutual covenants contained herein, the parties agree as follows:

SECTION ONE - DESCRIPTION OF PREMISES - Landlord leases to tenant premises on the _____ floor of the building known as "_____,"

Page 1 of 13

LEASE OF OFFICE SPACE - Continued

located at

_____
(Address)

_____
(City)

_____
(County)

_____
(State)

as shown on the _____ attached hereto as Exhibit "A".
                    (blueprint/diagram)

The premises shall be used for the purpose of _____
                                                (specify purpose)

_____,

and for no other purpose. The demised premises are located on commercial property

presently zoned for the following purposes: _____.
                                              (describe zoning)

This includes the purpose for which tenant desires the premises.

Landlord has provided tenant a copy of all documents describing the title,

access, and easements relating to the demised premises, and will provide a copy of

any subsequent document that may affect the rights of tenant herein.

SECTION TWO - TERM OF LEASE - The lease shall last for _____ years, to
                                                            (number)

commence on _____, 19____, and terminate on _____, 19____,
             (month and day)   (yr)   (month and day)   (yr)

unless tenant has exercised the option to renew under provisions set forth herein.

Tenant shall surrender the premises to landlord immediately on termination of the

lease.

LEASE OF OFFICE SPACE - Continued

SECTION THREE - DELIVERY OF POSSESSION - If, for any reason, landlord cannot

deliver possession of the premises at the commencement of the term, this lease

shall not be void or voidable, nor shall landlord be liable to tenant for any loss

or damage resulting therefrom. However, there shall be a proportionate reduction

in total rent, covering the period between the commencement of the term and actual

delivery of the premises to tenant, in the event of a late delivery by landlord.

SECTION FOUR - RENTAL - Tenant shall pay a total of _____ Dollars

($ _____) for the term of this lease, payable in _____ equal
                                                              (number)

monthly payments of _____ Dollars ($_____), due in advance on the

_____ day of each month for the succeeding month's rental. This sum
(number)

reflects a monthly rate of _____ Dollars ($_____) per

square foot of office space. Payments shall be made to landlord at the address

specified above, and a payment shall be delinquent if not paid by the

_____ day after which it is due. On tenant's failure to pay the rental
(number)

on a timely basis, landlord shall have the right to terminate this lease, and the

lease will thereupon be forfeited.

SECTION FIVE - RESTRICTIONS ON USE - Tenant shall not use or permit the premises,

or any part thereof, to be used for any purposes other than those set forth

herein. Tenant shall neither permit on the premises any act, sale, or storage

that may be prohibited under standard forms of fire insurance policies, nor use

the premises for any such purpose. In addition, no use shall be made or permitted

to be made that shall result in (1) waste on the premises, (2) a public or private

nuisance that may disturb the quiet enjoyment of other tenants in the building,

LEASE OF OFFICE SPACE - Continued

(3) improper, unlawful, or objectionable use, including sale, storage, or preparation, of food, alcoholic beverages, or materials generating an odor on the premises, or (4) noises or vibrations that may disturb other tenants. Tenant shall comply with all governmental regulations and statutes affecting the premises either now or in the future and shall also comply with the rules and regulations attached to this lease and made a part hereof.

SECTION SIX - ABANDONING PREMISES OR PERSONAL PROPERTY - Tenant shall not vacate or abandon the premises at any time during the term, but if tenant does vacate or abandon the premises or is dispossessed by process of law, any personal property belonging to tenant and left on the premises shall be deemed abandoned at the option of landlord and shall become the property of landlord.

SECTION SEVEN - TAXES - Landlord shall pay all real property taxes on the office building up to a maximum of _____ Dollars ($_____) per year. The excess of any real property tax assessment over that maximum amount will be payable by the tenants of the building in the same proportion that the area of office space each tenant is leasing bears to the total leased area of the building.

SECTION EIGHT - UTILITIES AND ELEVATORS - Landlord shall furnish all heat and air conditioning to the demised premises on all business days during the appropriate seasons, between the hours of _____ o'clock a.m. and _____ o'clock p.m.

Landlord shall furnish all electricity required by tenant in the normal conduct of business activities on the premises, but landlord shall be entitled to review the proposals of tenant to add any equipment requiring large electrical power supplies, and to charge tenant for the additional costs of the increased electrical service, if landlord deems the necessity therefor reasonable.

Page 4 of 13

LEASE OF OFFICE SPACE - Continued

Landlord shall furnish all hot and cold water for lavatory purposes without charge. If an additional supply of water is required by tenant, tenant shall install a water meter to register such additional consumption of water, and tenant shall pay as additional rent, when and as bills are received, the installation costs for the water meter, the costs for the additional water consumed, and for the sewer rents and all other rents and charges based on the added consumption of water by tenant.

Landlord _____ furnish passenger elevator service. If elevator
                (shall/shall not)

service is supplied, the hours of such service shall be from _____

o'clock a.m. to _____ o'clock p.m. There shall be _____
                                                                (number)

elevators available. There _____ be service available on
                            (shall/shall not)
Saturdays.

SECTION NINE - ALTERATIONS AND MODIFICATION; REPAIRS - Tenant has inspected the premises, and the premises are now in a tenantable and good condition. Tenant shall take good care of the premises and shall not alter, repair, or change the premises without the written consent of landlord. All alterations, improvements, and changes that tenant may desire shall be done either by or under the direction of landlord, but at the expense of tenant and shall become the property of landlord and remain on the premises, except that at the option of landlord, tenant shall, at tenant's expense, remove from the premises all partitions, counters, railings, and similarly installed improvements when surrendering the premises. All damage or injury done to the premises by tenant or any person who may be in or on the premises with the consent of tenant shall be paid for by tenant. Tenant shall, at the termination of this lease, surrender the premises to landlord in as good condition and repair as reasonable and proper use thereof will permit.

LEASE OF OFFICE SPACE - Continued

Landlord shall be responsible for making all routine repairs and for performing routine maintenance. Tenant shall permit landlord and landlord's agents to enter the premises at all reasonable times to inspect the premises, clean windows, perform other janitorial services, maintain the building and premises, and make repairs, alterations, or additions to the premises, or any portion of the building, including the erection of scaffolding, props, or other mechanical devices, to post notices of nonliability for alterations, additions, or repairs, or to place on the premises any usual or ordinary "For Sale" signs, without any rebate of rent to tenant or damages for any loss of occupation or quiet enjoyment of the premises. Landlord may, at any time within _____ days prior
(number)

to the expiration of this lease, place on the windows and doors of the premises any usual or ordinary "To Rent" or "To Lease" signs. Landlord and landlord's agents may, during the last-mentioned period, enter on the premises at reasonable hours, and exhibit the same to prospective tenants.

SECTION TEN - LIABILITY OF LANDLORD - Tenant waives all claims against landlord for damages to goods or for injuries to persons on or about the premises from any cause arising any time. Tenant will indemnify landlord on account of any damage or injury to any person, or to the goods of any person, arising from the use of the premises by tenant, or arising from the failure of tenant to keep the premises in good condition as provided herein. Landlord shall not be liable to tenant for any damage by or from any act or negligence of any other occupant of the same building, or by any owner or occupant of adjoining or continguous property. Tenant agrees to pay for all damage to the building, as well as all damage or injury suffered by tenants or occupants thereof caused by misuse or neglect of the premises by tenant.

LEASE OF OFFICE SPACE - Continued

SECTION ELEVEN - DESTRUCTION OF PREMISES - In the event of a partial destruction of the premises during the term from any cause, landlord shall forthwith repair the same, provided the repairs can be made within _____ days under
(number)

the laws and regulations of applicable governmental authorities. Any partial destruction shall neither annul not void this lease, except that tenant shall be entitled to a proportionate reduction of rent while the repairs are being made, any proportionate reduction being based on the extent to which the making of repairs shall interfere with the business carried on by tenant in the premises. If the repairs cannot by made in the specified time, landlord may, at landlord's option, make repairs within a reasonable time, this lease continuing in full force and effect and the rent to be proportionately rebated as previously set forth in this paragraph. In the event that landlord does not elect to make repairs that cannot be made in the specified time, or those repairs cannot be made under the laws and regulations of the applicable governmental authorities, this lease may be terminated at the option of either party. In the event of any partial destruction that landlord is obligated to repair or may elect to repair under the terms of this paragraph, the provisions of _____
(cite statute or as the case may be)

authorizing tenant to make the repairs and deduct the expenses from the rent are waived by tenant. Should the building in which the demised premises are situated be destroyed to the extent of not less than _____ per cent (_____%) of the replacement cost thereof, landlord may elect to terminate this lease, whether the demised premises are damaged or not. A total destruction of the building in which the premises are situated shall terminate this lease.

Any dispute between landlord and tenant relative to the provisions of those paragraphs shall be subject to arbitration. Each party shall select an arbitrator, and the two arbitrators so selected shall select a third arbitrator

Page 7 of 13

LEASE OF OFFICE SPACE - Continued

between them, the three arbitrators shall be final and binding on both landlord and tenant, who shall bear the cost of such arbitration equally between them.

SECTION TWELVE - CONDEMNATION - A condemnation of the entire building or a condemnation of the portion of the premises occupied by tenant shall result in a termination of this lease agreement. Lesssor shall receive the total of any consequential damages awarded as a result of condemnation proceedings. All future rent installments to be paid by tenant under this lease shall be terminated.

SECTION THIRTEEN - ASSIGNMENT AND SUBLEASE - Tenant shall not assign any right or duties under this lease nor sublet the premises or any part thereto, nor allow any other person to occupy or use the premises without the prior written consent of the landlord. A consent to one assignment, sublease, or occupation or use by any other person shall not be a consent to any subsequent assignment, sublease, or occupation or use by another person. Any assignment or subletting without consent shall be void. This lease shall not be assignable, as to the interest of tenant, by operation of law, without the written consent of landlord. Landlord shall not unreasonably withhold consent to assignment of sublease of the demised premises by tenant if tenant will provide evidence of the financial responsibility of the intended assignee of subtenant.

SECTION FOURTEEN - BREACH OR DEFAULT - Tenant shall have breached this lease and shall by considered in default hereunder if (1) tenant files a petition in bankruptcy or insolvency or for reorganization under any bankruptcy act, or makes an assignment for the benefit or creditors, (2) involuntary proceedings are instituted against tenant under any bankruptcy act, (3) tenant fails to pay any rent when due and does not make the delinquent payment within _____

(number)

LEASE OF OFFICE SPACE - Continued

days after receipt of notice thereof from landlord, or (4) tenant fails to perform

or comply with any of the covenants or conditions of this lease and such failure

continues for a period of _____ days after receipt of notice thereof
                          (number)

from landlord.

SECTION FIFTEEN - EFFECT OF BREACH - In the event of a breach of this lease as set

forth in SECTION FOURTEEN, the rights of landlord shall be as follows:

(1) Landlord shall have the right to cancel and terminate this lease, as well

as all of the right, title, and interest of tenant hereunder, by giving to tenant

not less than _____ days' notice of the cancellation and termination.
             (number)

On expiration of the time fixed in the notice, this lease and the right, title,

and interest of tenant hereunder shall terminate in the same manner and with the

same force and effect, except as to tenant's liability, as if the date fixed in

the notice of cancellation and termination were the end of the term herein

originally determined.

(2) Landlord may elect, but shall not be obligated, to make any payment

required of tenant herein or comply with any agreement, term, or condition

required hereby to be performed by tenant, and landlord shall have the right to

enter the demised premises for the purpose of correction or remedying any such

default and to remain until the default has been corrected or remedied, but any

expenditure for the correction by landlord shall not be deemed to waive or release

tenant's default or landlord's right to take any action as may be otherwise

permissible hereunder in the case of any default.

(3) Landlord may re-enter the premises immediately and remove the property and

personnel of tenant, and store the property in a public warehouse or at a place

selected by landlord, at the expense of tenant. After re-entry landlord may

Page 9 of 13

LEASE OF OFFICE SPACE - Continued

terminate the lease on giving _____ days' written notice of termination
(number)

to tenant. On termination landlord may recover from tenant all damages

proximately resulting from the breach, including the cost of recovering the

premises and the worth of the balance of this lease over the reasonable rental

value of the premises for the remainder of the lease term, which sum shall be

immediately due landlord from tenant.

After re-entry, landlord may re-rent the premises or any part thereof for any

term without termination the lease, at the rent and on the terms as landlord may

choose, Landlord may make alterations and repairs to the premises. The duties

and liabilities of the parties if the premises are re-rent as provided herein

shall be as follows:

(a) In addition to tenant's liability to landlord for breach of the lease, tenant

shall be liable for all expenses of the re-renting, for the alterations and

repairs made, and for the difference between the rent received by landlord

under the new lease agreement and the rent installments that are due for the

same period under this lease.

(b) Landlord shall have the right to apply the rent received from re-renting the

premises (1) to reduce tenant's indebtedness to landlord under the lease, not

including indebtedness for rent, (2) to expenses of the re-renting and

alterations and repairs made, (3) to rent due under this lease, or (4) to

payment of future rent under this lease as it becomes due.

If the new tenant does not pay a rent installment promptly to landlord, and

the rent installment has been credited in advance of payment to the

indebtedness of tenant other than rent, or if rentals from the new tenant

have been otherwise applied by landlord as provided for herein, and during

any rent installment period, are less than the rent payable for the

LEASE OF OFFICE SPACE - Continued

corresponding installment period under this lease, tenant shall pay landlord the deficiency, separately for each rent installment deficiency period and before the end of that period. Landlord may at any time after a re-renting terminate the lease for the breach on which landlord had based the re-entry and subsequently re-rent the premises.

(4) After re-entry, landlord may procure the appointment of a receiver to take possession and collect rents and profits of the business of tenant, and, if necessary to collect the rents and profits the receiver may carry on the business of tenant and take possession of the personal property used in the business of tenant, including inventory, trade fixtures, and furnishings, and use them in the business without compensating tenant. Proceedings for appointment of a receiver by landlord, or the appointment of a receiver and the conduct of the business of tenant by the receiver, shall not terminate and forfeit this lease unless landlord has given written notice of termination to tenant as provided herein.

SECTION SIXTEEN - OPTION TO RENEW - Tenant shall have the option to renew this lease _____ times for an identical term as provided herein for each
    (number)

renewal. Written notice of intention to renew must be furnished landlord

_____ days prior to expiration of the lease or any renewal hereunder.
(number)

The rental shall be subject to renegotiation at the time of any renewal, but all other terms and conditions shall remain as provided herein.

SECTION SEVENTEEN - UNLAWFUL DETAINER AND ATTORNEYS' FEES - In case suit shall be brought for an unlawful detainer of the premises, for the recovery of any rent due under the provisions of this lease, or for tenant's breach of any other condition

LEASE OF OFFICE SPACE - Continued

contained herein, tenant shall pay to landlord a reasonable attorneys' fee which shall be fixed by the court, and such attorneys' fee shall be deemed to have accrued on the commencement of the action and shall be paid on the successful completion of this action by landlord. Tenant shall be entitled to attorneys' fees in the same manner if judgment is rendered for tenant.

SECTION EIGHTEEN - SECURITY DEPOSIT - Tenant shall deposit _____ Dollars ($_____) with landlord's security for return of the premises in proper condition at the end of the lease term or on earlier termination and forfeiture as provided herein. Landlord may transfer or deliver the security to any bona fide purchaser of the real property in the event that the property is sold, and landlord shall be discharged from any further liability in reference to the security on giving written notice of that transfer to tenant.

SECTION NINETEEN - HOLDING OVER - If tenant holds possession of the premises after the term of this lease, tenant shall become a tenant from month to month on the terms herein specified, but at a monthly rental of _____ Dollars ($_____) per month payable monthly in advance on the _____
                                                                            (number)
day of each month, and tenant shall continue to be a month-to-month tenant until the tenancy shall be terminated by landlord, or until tenant has given to landlord a written notice at least one month prior to the date of termination of the monthly tenancy of tenant's intention to terminate the tenancy.

SECTION TWENTY - REMEDIES OF LANDLORD CUMULATIVE - The remedies herein given to landlord shall be cumulative, and the exercise of any one remedy by landlord shall not be to the exclusion of any other remedy.

LEASE OF OFFICE SPACE - Continued

In witness whereof, the parties have executed this lease in the City of

_____ , State of _____ ,

the day and the year first above written.

_____
(Signature of landlord)

_____
(Signature of landlord)

_____
(Signature of tenant)

_____
(Signature of tenant)

If required by state law, two witnesses for landlord and two witnesses for tenant should sign this agreement:

_____
(Witness for landlord)

_____
(Witness for landlord)

_____
(Witness for tenant)

_____
(Witness for tenant)

LEASE OF STORE

Agreement made _____ , 19___ , between:
       (month and day)   (yr)

_____   and   _____
(Name(s) of tenant)   (Name(s) of landlord)

herein referred to as tenant, of   herein referred to as landlord, of

_____   _____
(Address)   (Address)

_____   _____
(City)   (City)

_____   _____
(County)   (County)

_____   _____
(State)   (State)

RECITALS

1. Landlord is the owner of the developed property described below, and landlord desires to lease the property for use as a retail store.

2. Tenant desires to locate a retail store in the area of landlord's property.

In consideration of the mutual covenants contained herein, the parties agree as follows:

SECTION ONE - DESCRIPTION OF PREMISES - Landlord leases to tenant the premises located at _____
                                    (Address)

_____
(City)

_____
(County)

_____
(State)

LEASE OF STORE - Continued

and more particularly described as follows: _____
(insert legal description)

_____ ,

including dimensions, furnishings, trade fixtures (or as the case may be) as

follows: _____

_____

_____

_____

_____

_____

_____

_____ .

SECTION TWO - PURPOSE - Tenant shall use the demised premises for the exclusive

purpose of conducting a _____
(type of business, such as: retail hardware store)

thereon and shall conduct the business during all usual working hours for related

business activities, excepting therefrom periods when prevented by acts of God, or

other causes beyond the control of tenant. Tenant shall comply with all

governmental regulations affecting the operation of the demised premises in this

manner.

SECTION THREE - RESTRICTION ON USE - Lease shall not conduct any activity that is

unlawful, ultrahazardous, or that would increase the premiums for liability

insurance on the premises. All advertising material that is to be affixed to the

exterior portions of the building by tenant shall be submitted to landlord for

approval prior to installation, and all material installed shall be removed by

tenant on surrender of the premises.

Page 2 of 9

LEASE OF STORE - Continued

SECTION FOUR - RESERVATIONS BY LANDLORD - Landlord shall have the right to enter the premises at an reasonable hour to inspect the business records of tenant, and tenant's books, accounts, and records shall be available for such examination on reasonable demand. Landlord shall have the right to enter the premises to inspect the premises and make repairs, alterations, or modifications as required.

SECTION FIVE - TERM OF LEASE - The term of the lease shall be for _____
(number)

years, commencing _____, 19 ___, and terminating _____,
(month and day)   (yr)   (month and day)

19___, at _____ o'clock ____.m., unless renewed under the provisions of
(yr)

Section Twelve herein.

SECTION SIX - RENTAL - Tenant shall pay _____ Dollars ($_____) basic rental for the term of the lease for the demised premises at the rate of _____ Dollars ($_____) per month. The monthly rental payment shall be due on the _____ day of each month for the succeeding month's rental.

Cross out either Paragraph A or Paragraph B:

A) Tenant shall pay a percentage rental in addition to the basic rental provided herein of _____ per cent (_____%) of gross receipts, which shall be payable each month, _____days after the close of the accounting month of lease.

OR

B) Tenant shall pay no percentage rental in addition to the basic rental provided for herein.

Page 3 of 9

LEASE OF STORE - Continued

SECTION SEVEN - DAMAGES - Tenant shall give notice to landlord of damages caused by natural disasters, and landlord shall repair the damages within _____ (number)

days, during which time tenant shall be entitled to an abatement on the rental.

Where more than _____ per cent (_____%) of the demised premises is destroyed by a natural disaster, landlord shall have the option of refusing to repair or replace the premises, and the duty to pay rental under this lease shall terminate as of the date of the disaster.

Tenant shall be liable for the costs of all damages caused by the negligence of tenant, and there will be no abatement of rent or termination of this lease for these damages.

SECTION EIGHT - UTILITES- Tenant shall be responsible for paying the following utilities or services connected with the premises (check those applicable):

_____ water   _____ phone

_____ sewer   _____ trash pick up

_____ electricity   _____ Other: _____

_____ gas   _____ Other: _____

Landlord shall arrange and grant all necessary easements to utility service suppliers to facilitate installation, maintenance, and repairing of utility service required by tenant.

SECTION NINE - TAXES - Landlord shall pay all real property taxed and assessments levied on the original premises in an amount up to and including _____ Dollars (_____$) per year. This amount was established by using 19_____ as (yr)

the base year for tax assessment. All taxes levied over and above that amount on

Page 4 of 9

LEASE OF STORE - Continued

the premises as existing at the commencement of this lease shall be paid by tenant. Any increase in real property taxed or assessments occasioned by alteration, addition, or modification to the premises shall be apportioned among the parties as follows: _____

_____ .

Tenant shall pay all personal property taxes and assessments and all business taxes and license fees.

SECTION TEN - ASSIGNMENT AND SUBLEASE - Tenant shall not assign this lease or sublet the premises to another party without the express written approval or landlord.

SECTION ELEVEN - REPAIRS, ALTERATIONS, AND MODIFICATIONS - Landlord shall be responsible for all repairs to the common areas, accesses, service entrances, parking areas, and the exterior of the building, all repairs necessitated by faulty workmanship in the construction of the building, and all repairs necessitated by casualty losses covered by casualty insurance provided herein. Tenant shall be responsible for all repairs required as a result of the negligent acts of tenant or its agents and all repairs not required of landlord. All normal maintenace of the premises will be carried out to suit tenant's needs, provided that written consent of landlord has first been obtained.

SECTION TWELVE - OPTION TO RENEW - Tenant shall have the option to renew this agreement for _____
                 (another term equal to the term hereof or as the case may be)
at a rental rate of _____ Dollars ($_____) per month, with all other terms and conditions of the renewal lease to be the same as those

LEASE OF STORE - Continued

herein.   Tenant may exercise this option by giving written notice to landlord at

least _____ days before expiration of this agreement.
      (number)

SECTION THIRTEEN - FINANCIAL STATEMENT OF TENANT - Cross out either Paragraph A or

Paragraph B:

  A)   Tenant shall provide a monthly statement of gross receipts to landlord by

       the _____ day of each month. The percentage rental rate, if
           (number)

       any, shall be calculated on this monthly figure. Landlord may have the

       books and records of tenant audited at tenant's expense if landlord is

       dissatisfied with the statement furnished by tenant.

                                   OR

  B)   Tenant shall not provide monthly statements of gross receipts to

       landlord.

SECTION FOURTEEN - INSURANCE - Tenant shall carry fire and any other casualty

insurance generally carried on a business of this nature on the demised premises

during the term of this lease in an amount equal to _____ per cent

(_____%) of the appraised value of the insured property, written by a reliable

insurer in the name of landlord and tenant in proportion to their respective

interest in the demised premises. Tenant shall furnish liability insurance in the

amounts of _____ Dollars ($_____) for each injury to either

employees or invitees on the business premises, _____ Dollars

($_____) for each accident or occurrence, and _____ Dollars

($_____) for property damage. Landlord may purchase these policies and

charge tenant therefor if tenant fails to comply with this requirement.

Page 6 of 9

LEASE OF STORE - Continued

Landlord and tenant, together and separately, waive any right of subrogation or any right in tort against the other party, party's agents or assigns, for damages to the premises or to persons in excess of the insurance policy provisions herein.

SECTION FIFTEEN - BANKRUPTCY - Landlord shall have the option on
(number)
days' notice to tenant to terminate this lease agreement in the event tenant files for voluntary bankruptcy, is placed in receivership, or has involuntary bankruptcy proceedings instituted against tenant by creditors.

SECTION SIXTEEN - CONDEMNATION - This lease agreement shall terminate in the event of a total condemnation by an authorized governmental agency. A partial condemnation shall only terminate the lease at the option of landlord, but if landlord elects to continue the lease, tenant shall be entitled to a partial abatement of rent proportionate to the loss of use in the premises suffered by tenant. Landlord shall be entitled to all consequential damages awarded as a result of any eminent domain proceedings.

SECTION SEVENTEEN - EXAMINATION OF PREMISES - Tenants shall examine the premises prior to execution of this lease and shall acknowledge that the demised premises are in satisfactory condition at the time tenant enters into possession of the premises. Landlord has made no representations to tenant relating to the condition of the premises except as provided in this lease agreement.

SECTION EIGHTEEN - DEFAULT AND FORFEITURE - Landlord shall, on default with respect to any of the provisions of this lease by tenant, provide tenant with written notice of any breach of the lease terms or conditions and tenant shall

LEASE OF STORE - Continued

then have _____ days to either correct the condition, or commence
         (number)

corrective action if the condition cannot be corrected in _____ days,
                                                          (number)

tenant shall have a reasonable time to complete the correction. Landlord may

elect to enforce the terms and conditions of the lease by any other method

available under the law, or landlord may declare a forfeiture of the lease by

providing _____ days' notice to tenant of landlord's intent to do so.
          (number)

SECTION NINETEEN - HOLDING OVER - Tenant shall pay to landlord a monthly sum equal

to the rent specified in this lease plus _____ per cent (_____%)

thereof for each month that tenant holds the premises after expiration or

termination of this lease without authorization by landlord. This sum shall be

liquidated damages for the wrongful holding over. Tenant shall acquire no

additional rights, title, or interest to the demised premises by holding the

premises after termination or expiration of this agreement and shall be subject to

legal action by landlord to obtain the removal of tenant.

SECTION TWENTY - REMEDIES FOR LANDLORD - Any and all remedies provided to landlord

for the enforcement of the provisions of this lease are cumulative and not

exclusive, and landlord shall be entitled to pursue either the rights enumerated

in this lease or remedies authorized by law, or both. Tenant shall be liable for

any costs or expenses incurred by landlord in enforcing any terms of this lease,

or in pursuing any legal action for the enforcement of landlord's rights.

LEASE OF STORE - Continued

In witness whereof, the parties have executed this lease in the City of

_____ , State of _____ , the

day and the year first above written.

_____
(Signature of landlord)

_____
(Signature of landlord)

_____
(Signature of tenant)

_____
(Signature of tenant)

If required by state law, two witnesses for landlord and two witnesses for tenant
should sign this agreement:

_____
(Witness for landlord)

_____
(Witness for landlord)

_____
(Witness for tenant)

_____
(Witness for tenant)

SUBLEASE OF OFFICE SPACE

Agreement made _____, 19___, between:
　　　　　　　　(month and day)　　　　　　　　 (yr)

_____　and　　_____
(Name(s) of tenant)　　　　　　　　　　　(Name(s) of subtenant)

herein referred to as tenant, of　　　herein referred to as subtenant, of

_____　　　　　　_____
(Address)　　　　　　　　　　　　　　　(Address)

_____　　　　　　_____
(City)　　　　　　　　　　　　　　　　 (City)

_____　　　　　　_____
(County)　　　　　　　　　　　　　　　 (County)

_____　　　　　　_____
(State)　　　　　　　　　　　　　　　　(State)

RECITALS

1. Tenant has leased space in an office building.

2. Subtenant desires to obtain office space in the geographical area in which the
    building is located.

3. The parties desire to enter a sublease agreement defining all rights, duties,
    and liabilities of the parties hereto.

    In consideration of the mutual covenants contained herein, the parties agree
as follows:

SECTION ONE - DESCRIPTION OF PREMISES - Tenant has leased a building consisting of
_____ floors and approximately _____ square feet of
office space from _____, herein known as landlord,

SUBLEASE OF OFFICE SPACE - Continued

which is located at

_____
(Address)

_____
(City)

_____
(County)

_____.
(State)

Tenant shall demise to subtenant _____ square feet of the
                                          (number)

building, all located on the _____ floor, as more fully described in
                                  (number)

Exhibit "A" attached hereto.

SECTION TWO - PURPOSE OF SUBLEASE - The premises demised under this sublease are

to be used by subtenant in the conduct of the business of _____
                                                              (describe subtenant's

_____,
business)

and all tasks related thereto. Subtenant shall not use the premises for any

illegal, immoral, or ultrahazardous activity, whether within or outside the scope

of the business of subtenant.

SECTION THREE - TERM OF SUBLEASE - The term of this sublease shall be for an

initial period of _____ years, commencing on _____,

19____, and terminating on _____, 19 ____, unless sooner terminated

by breach of the terms and conditions of this agreement or as provided in SECTIONS

SEVEN or SIXTEEN hereof. Landlord concurs that subtenant may remain in possession

of the premises for the full term of this sublease, despite any change that may

occur in the status of tenant or the lease between tenant and landlord.

SUBLEASE OF OFFICE SPACE - Continued

SECTION FOUR - RENT - Subtenant shall pay to tenant as basic rent _____ Dollars ($_____) per month, on the _____ day of each month
(number)
thereafter during the term of this sublease, and subtenant shall pay all other sums due as additional rental under the provisions of this sublease on the basic rental payment due date first occurring after the additional rental payment arises.

SECTION FIVE - UTILITES- Tenant shall be responsible for paying the following utilities or services connected with the premises (check those applicable):

_____ water		_____ phone	
_____ sewer		_____ trash pick up	
_____ electricity		_____ Other: _____	
_____ gas		_____ Other: _____	

Subtenant shall be responsible for the following utilities or services:

_____
(list utilities or services)

_____

_____.

SECTION SIX - ACCIDENTAL DAMAGE OR INJURY - Landlord and tenant shall not be liable for any damage to property or any injury to persons, sustained by subtenant or others, caused by conditions or activities on the premises. Subtenant shall indemnify landlord and tenant against all claims arising therefrom and shall carry liability insurance insuring tenant, subtenant, and landlord against any claims in amounts to be approved by landlord.

SUBLEASE OF OFFICE SPACE - Continued

SECTION SEVEN - CASUALTY DAMAGE OR INJURY - If the premises shall be destroyed or damaged by any acts of war, the elements, including earthquake, or fire, to such an extent as to render the premises untenantable in whole or in substantial part, landlord has the option of rebuilding or repairing the premises by giving notice to that effect to tenant within _____ days after the occurrence of
(number)
any damage, of the intent of landlord to rebuild or repair the premises or the part so damaged. If landlord elects to rebuild or repair the premises and does so without unnecessary delay, subtenant shall be bound by this lease, except that during the period of repair, the rent of the premises shall be abated in the same proportion that the portion of the premises rendered unfit for occupancy by subtenant shall bear to the whole of the subleased premises. If landlord fails to give notice of the intent to repair, subtenant shall have the right to declare this sublease terminated.

SECTION EIGHT - COMPLIANCE WITH ORIGINAL LEASE AND LAWS - Subtenant shall not cause or allow any undue waste on the premises and shall comply with all applicable laws and ordinances respecting the use and occupancy of the premises relating to matters not covered elsewhere in this sublease, provided that subtenant shall not be required to make any alterations, additions, or improvements to the premises in order to conform with this sublease.

Subtenant shall perform, and observe the terms and conditions to be performed on the part of the tenant under the provisions of the original lease between tenant and landlord, excepting the covenant for the payment of rent reserved thereby, and to indemnify tenant against all claims, damages, costs, and expenses in respect to the nonperformance or nonobservance of any such terms or conditions.

SUBLEASE OF OFFICE SPACE - Continued

SECTION NINE - REPAIRS - Subject to the obligations of landlord under SECTION _____ of the original lease, tenant, unless herein specified to the
(number)

contrary, shall maintain the premises in good repair and tenantable condition

during the continuance of this sublease, except in case of damage arising from

acts or negligence of subtenant or the agents of subtenant.

SECTION TEN - ALTERATIONS, ADDITIONS, OR IMPROVEMENTS - Subtenant shall not make

any alterations, additions, or improvements on or to the premises without first

obtaining the written consent of tenant, and all alterations, additions, and

improvements that shall be made shall be at the sole expense of subtenant and

shall become the property of tenant and shall remain on and be surrendered with

the premises as a part thereof at the termination of this sublease without

disturbance, molestation, or injury. Nothing contained in this provision shall

prevent subtenant from removing all office machines, equipment, and trade fixtures

customarily used in the business of subtenant.

SECTION ELEVEN - LIENS - Subtenant shall keep the subleased premises free and

clear of all liens arising out of any work performed, materials furnished, or

obligations incurred by subtenant.

SECTION TWELVE - ACCESS TO PREMISES - Subtenant shall allow landlord or tenant or

the agents or employees of either the free access to premises at all reasonable

times for the purpose of inspection of making repairs, additions, or alterations

to the premises or any property owned by or under the control of either party.

SECTION THIRTEEN - ADVERTISEMENTS - All signs or symbols placed in the windows or

doors of the premises, or on any exterior part of the building by subtenant, shall

be subject to the approval of tenant. If subtenant shall place signs or symbols

SUBLEASE OF OFFICE SPACE - Continued

on the exterior of the building or in windows or doors where they are visible from the street that are not satisfactory to tenant, tenant may immediately demand the removal of the signs or symbols, and the refusal by subtenant to comply with any demand within a period of _____ hours will constitute a breach of
(number)

this sublease and entitle tenant immediately to recover possession of the premises in the manner provided by law. Any signs so placed on the premises shall be so placed on the understanding and agreement that subtenant shall remove these signs or symbols at the termination of the tenancy herein created and repair any damage or injury to the premises caused thereby. If not so removed by subtenant, then tenant may have the signs or symbols removed at the expence of the subtenant.

SECTION FOURTEEN - SALES, ASSIGNMENTS, AND SUBLEASES - Subtenant shall not assign this sublease, or sell or sublet the premises subleased herein, or any part thereof of interest herein, without the prior written consent of tenant. This sublease shall not be assigned by operation of law. If consent is once given by tenant to the assignment of this sublease or sublease of the premises or any interest therein, tenant shall not be barred from subsequently refusing to consent to any further assignment of sublease. Any attempt to sell, assign, or sublet without the consent of tenant, shall be deemed as a default by subtenant, entitling tenant to re-enter pursuant to SECTION NINETEEN if tenant so elects.

SECTION FIFTEEN - QUIET ENJOYMENT - If subtenant performs the terms of this sublease, tenant will warrant and defend subtenant in the enjoyment and peaceful possession of the premises during the term hereof without any interruption by tenant or landlord or either of them or any person rightfully claiming under either of them.

SUBLEASE OF OFFICE SPACE - Continued

SECTION SIXTEEN - CONDEMNATION - If the premises or any part thereof are appropriated or taken for any public use by virtue of eminent domain or condemnation proceedings, or if by reason of law, ordinance, or by court decree, whether by consent or otherwise, the use of the premises by subtenant for any of the specific purposes referred to herein shall be prohibited, subtenant shall have the right to terminate this lease on written notice to tenant, and rental shall be paid only to the time when sublease surrenders possession of the premises. In the event of partial appropriation, subtenant may elect to continue in possession of that part of the premises not so appropriated under the same terms and conditions hereof, except that in these cases subtenant shall be entitled to an equitable reduction of the rental payment hereunder. Any rental paid in advance beyond the time that the property has been taken from subtenant shall be returned by tenant to subtenant on demand. Subtenant does not waive any right to recover from the condemnation authority for any damage that may be suffered by subtenant by reason of any condemnation.

SECTION SEVENTEEN - OPTION TO RENEW - Subject to the receipt by tenant of an extention of the original lease for a sufficient duration to include this renewal, at any time before the commencement of the last calendar month of the first term of this sublease, subtenant is granted the option and privilege of extending and renewing the term of this sublease for an additional _____ year period
(number)
at an annual rental to be agreed on or arbitrated as provided herein.

SECTION EIGHTEEN - DEFAULT BY LANDLORD OR TENANT - If landlord or tenant fails or neglects to perform the sublease or the provisions of the original lease between them, then subtenant may, after reasonable notice in writing of not less than _____ days, terminate this sublease.
(number)

SUBLEASE OF OFFICE SPACE - Continued

SECTION NINETEEN - DEFAULT OF SUBTENANT - If any rent is reserved, or any part thereof, shall be and remain unpaid when these rents shall become due, or if subtenant violates or defaults in any of the provisions of this sublease, then tenant may cancel this sublease by giving the notice required herein, and re-enter the premises. Notwithstanding any re-entry, the liability of subtenant for the rent shall not be extinguished for the balance of the term hereof, and subtenant shall make good to tenant any deficiency arising from a re-entry and re-renting of the premises at a reduced rental. Subtenant shall pay any deficiency on the first day of each month immediately following the month in which the amount of deficiency is ascertained by tenant.

SECTION TWENTY - INSOLVENCY OR BANKRUPTCY - If subtenant becomes insolvent, voluntarily or involuntarily bankrupt, or if a receiver, assignee, or other liquidation officer is appointed for the business of subtenant, than tenant may terminate this sublease at the option of tenant.

SECTION TWENTY-ONE - WAIVER OF BREACH - The waiving of any of the provisions of this lease by any party shall be limited to the particular instance involved and shall not be deemed to waive any other rights of the same or any other terms of this sublease.

SECTION TWENTY-TWO - TERMINATION AND SURRENDER - Subtenant shall surrender the premises within _____ days from receipt of notice of termination of
(number)
this sublease, or on the last day of the term of the sublease. Tenant shall have the right to place and maintain on the premises "For Rent" or "For Sale" signs during the last _____ days of the term of this sublease.
(number)
Subtenant shall, at the expiration of this sublease, surrender the keys to the premises to tenant.

SUBLEASE OF OFFICE SPACE - Continued

SECTION TWENTY-THREE - REMOVAL OF PERSONAL PROPERTY - Subtenant shall have the right to remove all personal property, trade fixtures, and office equipment, whether attached to the premises or not, provided that these items can be removed without serious damage to the building or premises. All holes or damages to the building or premises caused by removal of any items shall be restored or repaired by subtenant promptly. Subtenant shall be entitled to remove any electrical service connections installed by subtenant that were designed specifically for subtenant.

If tenant or landlord re-enter or re-take possession of the premises prior to normal expiration of this sublease, tenant or landlord shall have the right, but not the obligation, to remove from the premises all personal property located therein belonging to subtenant, and either party may place the property in storage in a public warehouse at the expense and risk of subtenant.

SECTION TWENTY-FOUR - HOLDING OVER - Any holding over at the expiration of this sublease with the consent of tenant shall be on a month-to-month basis, which tenancy may thereafter by terminated as provided by the laws of the State of

_____. During any holdover tenancy, subtenant shall pay the same rate of rental on a monthly basis as is in effect at the time of the termination of this sublease and shall be bound by all the terms and conditions of this sublease.

SECTION TWENTY-FIVE - INTEREST OF SUCCESSORS - The convenants and agreements of this sublease shall be binding on the successors and assigns of tenant and on the successors and assigns of subtenant but only to the extent herein specified.

SUBLEASE OF OFFICE SPACE - Continued

SECTION TWENTY-SIX - NOTICES - Except where otherwise required by statute, all notices given pursuant to the provisions hereof may be sent by certified mail, postage prepaid, to the last known mailing address of the party of whom the notice is intended.

SECTION TWENTY-SEVEN - ARBITRATION - If any controversy develops that is to be submitted to arbitration according to the terms of this sublease, it shall be arbitrated in accordance with the arbitration laws of the State of _____, as supplemented by the current rules of the American Arbitration Association. Judgment on any award rendered may be entered in any court having jurisdiction over the parties and the property.

SECTION TWENTY-EIGHT - COSTS OF LITIGATION - If any legal action is instituted to enforce this sublease, or any part hereof, the prevailing party shall be entitled to recover reasonable attorneys' fees and court costs from the other party.

SECTION TWENTY-NINE - VENUE - At the option of either party, venue of any action may be established in _____
(County)

_____.
(State)

Personal service either within or without the State of _____ shall be sufficient to give that court jurisdiction.

SECTION THIRTY - ACKNOWLEDGEMENT BY LANDLORD - The foregoing sublease is made with the full knowledge and agreement of landlord of the premises, and landlord accepts the sublease herein but retains all rights to disapprove any future sublease or between tenant and any other party.

SUBLEASE OF OFFICE SPACE - Continued

In witness whereof, the parties have executed this lease in the City of

_____ , State of _____ ,

the day and the year first above written.

_____   _____
(Signature of tenant)   (Signature of subtenant)

_____   _____
(Signature of tenant)   (Signature of subtenant)

If required by state law, two witnesses for tenant and two witnesses for subtenant

should sign this agreement:

_____   _____
(Witness for landlord   (Witness fo tenant)

_____   _____
(Witness for landlord   (Witness fo tenant)

Page 11 of 11

SUBLEASE: SHORT FORM

Sublease made _____, 19____, between:
           (month and day)   (yr)

_____ and _____
(Name(s) of tenant)   (Name(s) of subtenant)

herein referred to as tenant, of   herein referred to as subtenant, of

_____   _____
(Address)   (Address)

_____   _____
(City)   (City)

_____   _____
(County)   (County)

_____   _____
(State)   (State)

and

_____
(Name(s) of landlord)

herein referred to as landlord, of

_____
(Address)

_____
(City)

_____
(County)

_____.
(State)

SUBLEASE: SHORT FORM - Continued

RECITALS

1. Landlord, by lease dated _____, 19____, leased to tenant the
                                                (month and day)   (yr)

    premises located at _____
                               (Address)

                               _____
                               (City)

                               _____
                               (County)

                               _____.
                               (State)

    and more particularly described as follows: _____
                                              (insert legal description)

    _____.

2. The lease provides that tenant shall not sublet the premises, or any part thereof, or assign the lease or any interest therein without the consent of the landlord.

3. Tenant and subtenant desire that landlord consent to a sublease of the whole of the above-described premises.

    In consideration of the mutual covenants contained herein, the parties agree as follows:

    Landlord consents to the sublease requested, provided that subtenant shall be bound by each and every covenant and condition contained in the lease, a copy of which is attached hereto as Exhibit "A".

    Subtenant shall perform all the covenants and conditions contained in the lease to be performed by tenant except the payment of rent to be made by tenant to

SUBLEASE: SHORT FORM - Continued

landlord, and subtenant shall be and is bound by each and every covenant and condition contained in this lease.

Neither the subleasing of the above-described premises nor anything contained in this agreement shall release tenant from the obligation to perform and be bound by all the covenants and conditions contained in the lease.

In witness whereof, the parties have executed this sublease in the City of

_____, State of _____,

the day and the year first above written.

_____
(Signature of landlord)

_____
(Signature of tenant)

_____
(Signature of landlord)

_____
(Signature of tenant)

_____
(Signature of subtenant)

_____
(Signature of subtenant)

If required by state law, two witnesses for landlord and two witnesses for tenant and two witneses for subtenant should sign this agreement:

_____
(Witness for landlord)

_____
(Witness for tenant)

_____
(Witness for landlord)

_____
(Witness for tenant)

_____
(Witness for subtenant)

_____
(Witness for subtenant)

Page 3 of 3

CONSTRUCTION

AGREEMENT FOR CONSTRUCTION OF DWELLING: SHORT FORM

Agreement made _____, 19____ between:
              (month and day)   (yr)

_____ and   _____
(Name of owner)   (Name of contractor)

herein known as owner, of   herein known as contractor, of

_____   _____
(Address)   (Address)

_____   _____
(City)   (City)

_____   _____
(County)   (County)

_____   _____
(State)   (State)

Owner and contractor in consideration of the mutual covenants hereinafter set forth, agree as follows:

SECTION ONE - STRUCTURE AND SITE- Contractor shall furnish all labor and materials necessary to construct a _____ bedroom, _____
                      (number)   (model)

model, _____ upon the following described property, which
       (type of structure)

owner warrants owner owns, free and clear of lein and encumbrances: _____

_____
(legal description of property)

_____.

Page 1 of 4

CONSTRUCTION OF DWELLING: SHORT FORM - Continued

SECTION TWO - PLANS- Contractor shall construct the structure in conformance with the plans, specifications, and breakdown-and-binder receipt signed by the contractor and owner, and will do so in a workmanlike manner. Contractor is not responsible for furnishing any improvements other than the structure, such as landscaping, grading, walkways, painting, sewer or water systems, steps, driveways, patios and aprons, etc., unless they are specifically stated in the breakdown.

SECTION THREE - PAYMENT- Owner shall pay contractor the sum of

_____ Dollars ($_____) in installments as set forth in the escrow instructions or the primary lender's schedule (whichever is applicable) signed by owner. In the event any installment is not paid when due, contractor may stop work until payment is made and for _____ days thereafter.
(number)

In the event any installment is not paid within _____ days
(number)

after it is due, contractor may take such action as may be necessary, including legal proceedings, to enforce its rights hereunder.

SECTION FOUR - PREPARATION- Prior to the start of construction, owner shall provide a clear, accessible building site, properly excavated and correctly zoned for the structure, and shall identify the boundries of owner's property by stakes at all corners. Owner shall maintain such stakes in proper position throughout construction. In the event contractor cannot obtain a building permit within

_____ days of the date of this agreement, contractor may declare
(number)

the agreement of no further force or effect.

Page 2 of 4

CONSTRUCTION OF DWELLING: SHORT FORM - Continued

SECTION FIVE - UTILITIES-   Prior to the start of construction, and at all times during construction, owner shall provide and maintain, at owner's sole expense, an all-weather roadway to the building site, and water and electrical service, including 220 amp outlet. Owner shall, at owner's expense, connect permanent electrical service, gas service or oil service (whichever is applicable), and tanks and lines to the structure upon acceptable cover inspection and prior to wall covering. Owner shall, at owner's expense, connect sewage disposal and water lines to the structure within _____ days after the rough plumbing
(number)
is complete.

SECTION SIX - RESPONSIBILITY-   Contractor shall not be responsible for claims arising out of improper placement or positioning of boundry stakes or house stakes, and for damage to existing walks, driveways, cesspools, septic tanks, sewer lines, arches, shrubs, lawns, trees, telephone and electric lines and other property incurred in performance of the work or delivery of materials for construction; nor shall contractor be responsible for damages to persons or property occasioned by owner or owner's agents, third parties, acts of God or other causes beyond contractor's control. Owner shall hold contractor completely harmless from, and shall indemnify contractor for, all costs, damages, losses, and expenses, including judgements and attorneys' fees, resulting from claims arising from causes enumerated in this paragraph.

SECTION SEVEN - POSSESSION-   Owner shall not have possession of the structure until such time as all payments or other obligations required of them as set forth in this agreement have been fully paid or performed by them. If possession of

CONSTRUCTION OF DWELLING: SHORT FORM - Continued

structure is taken by owner before the above obligations are met, without the written consent of contractor, it shall be considered as acceptance of the structure, by the owner, as complete and satisfactory.

SECTION EIGHT - GENERAL PROVISIONS-   Owner agrees to prompty complete the necessary requirements to obtain financing and to prepare the site for construction.   In the event owner has not secured acceptable financing and/or has not properly met the site preparation requirements by _____, 19____,
                                                                        (month and day)   (yr)
owner agrees that the agreement price will be adjusted to the current price list in effect at the time the financing and lot preparation requirements are met.

There are no understandings or agreements between contractor and owner other than those set forth in this agreement and in the documents referred to in SECTIONS TWO and THREE. No other statement, representation or promise has been made to induce either party to enter into this agreement. This agreement and the documents referred to in SECTIONS TWO and THREE may not be modified or amended except by written agreement of the parties.

In witness whereof, the parties have executed this agreement in the City of _____, State of _____, on the day and year first written above.

_____   _____
(Signature of owner)   (Signature of contractor)

CONTRACT FOR CONSTRUCTION OF BUILDING: SHORT FORM

Agreement made _____, 19___, between:
(month and day)   (yr)

_____   and   _____
(Name of owner)   (Name of contractor)

herein known as owner, of   herein known as contractor, or

_____   _____
(Address)   (Address)

_____   _____
(City)   (City)

_____   _____
(County)   (County)

_____   _____
(State)   (State)

In consideration of the mutual covenants herein contained, the owner and contractor agree as follows:

SECTION ONE - CONTRACT DOCUMENTS- The contract documents consist of this agreement, conditions of the contract (general, supplementary and other conditions), drawings, specifications, all addenda issued prior to execution of this agreement and all modifications issued subsequent thereto. These form the contract, and all are as fully a part of the contract as if attached to this agreement or repeated herein. An enumeration of the contract documents appears in SECTION EIGHT.

SECTION TWO - DESCRIPTION OF WORK-

Contractor shall perform all the work required by the contract documents for

_____ Dollars ($_____). Said work shall consist

of _____
(general description of the work)

Page 1 of 4

CONSTRUCTION OF BUILDING: SHORT FORM - Continued

_____

_____

_____.

SECTION THREE - ARCHITECT-   The architect for this contract is

_____, of
(name of architect)

        _____
        (Address)

        _____
        (City)

        _____
        (County)

        _____.
        (State)

SECTION FOUR - TIME OF COMMENCEMENT AND COMPLETION-   The work to be performed

under this contract shall be commenced _____
                          (insert specific provisions)

_____

_____

_____

and completed _____
          (insert date or specific provisions)

_____

_____

_____

_____.

Special provisions for liquidating damages relating to failure to complete on

time are as follows (if none, cross out): _____

CONSTRUCTION OF BUILDING: SHORT FORM - Continued

_____

_____.

SECTION FIVE - PAYMENT- Owner shall pay contractor for the performance of the work, subject to additions and deductions by change order as provided in the conditions of the contract, in current funds, the contract sum of

_____ Dollars ($_____).

SECTION SIX - PROGRESS PAYMENTS- Based upon applications for payment submitted to the architect by contractor and certificates for payment issued by architect, owner shall make progress payments on account of the contract sum to the contractor as provided in the conditions of the contract as follows:

On or about the _____ day of each month, _____ per cent
                        (number)

(_____%) of the proportion of the contract sum properly allocable to labor, materials and equipment incorporated in the work and _____ per cent (_____%) of the portion of the contract sum properly allocable to materials and equipment suitably stored at the site or at some other location agreed upon in writing by the parties, up to the _____ day of that month, less the
                                              (number)

aggregate of previous payments in each case; and upon substantial completion of the entire work, a sum sufficient to increase the total payments to _____ per cent (_____%) of the contract sum, less such retainages as architect shall determine for all incomplete work and unsettled claims. Provisions made for limiting or reducing the amount retained after the work reaches a certain stage of completion are as follows (if none, cross out):

_____

CONSTRUCTION OF BUILDING: SHORT FORM - Continued

_____

_____ .

SECTION SEVEN - FINAL PAYMENT- Final payment, constituting the entire unpaid balance of the contract sum, shall be paid by owner to contractor _____
(number)

days after substantial completion of the work unless otherwise stipulated in the certificate of substantial completion, provided the work has then been completed, the contract fully performed, and a final certificate for payment has been issued by architect.

SECTION EIGHT - OTHER PROVISIONS-

A.   Terms used in the agreement which are defined in the conditions of the contract shall have the meanings designated in those conditions.

B.   The contract documents, which constitute the entire agreement between the owner and contractor, are listed in SECTION ONE, and except for modifications issued after the execution of this document, are enumerated as follows:

　　1.   Insert the agreement, conditions of the contract (general, supplementary, and any other conditions), drawings, specifications, addenda and accepted alternates, showing page or sheet numbers in all cases and dates where applicable.

　　2.   Insert any other provisions the parties deem desirable or necessary.

In witness whereof, the parties have executed this agreement in the City of _____, State of _____, on the day and year first above written.

_____   _____
(Signature of owner)   (Signature of contractor)

Page 4 of 4

RESIDENTIAL CONTRACT TO BUY AND SELL REAL ESTATE:
RESIDENCE TO BE ERECTED
(Seller's remedy limited to liquidated damages)

Agreement made _____ , 19____ , between:
_____(month and day)_____   __(yr)__

_____   and   _____
(Name(s) of seller)   (Name(s) of purchaser)

herein known as seller, of   herein known as purchaser, of

_____   _____
(Address)   (Address)

_____   _____
(City)   (City)

_____   _____
(County)   (County)

_____   _____
(State)   (State)

RECEIVED FROM _____ the sum of
_____(name of person(s) or entity providing earnest money)_____

_____ Dollars ($_____) evidenced by

_____ , to be held in a trust account
(personal check, cashier's check, promissory note)

with _____ as a deposit and part payment on the
_____(name of bank)_____

purchase of the following described real property improvements situated in

_____
(County)

_____
(State)

which is more particularly described as follows: _____
_____(legal description)_____

_____

_____

CONTRACT FOR RESIDENCE TO BE ERECTED - Continued

together with all improvements to be erected or presently erected thereon, thereinafter referred to as property, which purchaser agrees to buy and seller agrees to sell for a price of _____ Dollars ($_____).

SECTION ONE - PURCHASE PRICE- The total purchase price for said property shall be _____ Dollars ($_____), which shall be paid as follows: the sum of _____ Dollars ($_____)
<u>(amount of earnest money)</u>
hereby receipted for; and the balance of _____ Dollars ($_____) of the purchase price and any and all closing costs, in cash or certified funds at the time of closing and delivery of deed.

This agreement is contingent upon purchaser obtaining a first mortgage loan, as evidenced by a loan commitment in the amount of _____ Dollars ($_____) for a term of not less than _____ years, with
<u>(number)</u>
interest at the rate of not more than _____ per cent (%_____) per annum. Said loan is to be secured by the property hereinabove described, and purchaser covenants to apply for said loan within _____ days from the
<u>(number)</u>
date hereof and pursue said application diligently, pay all fees and furnish all information without delays.

If purchaser's application for said loan is rejected, seller shall have the right to process the application through mortgages of seller's choice, not, however, to exceed three in number, and purchaser agrees to apply to any mortgagee designated by seller after such notification and pursue said application diligently. In the event that purchaser's application is rejected by all

Page 2 of 10

CONTRACT FOR RESIDENCE TO BE ERECTED - Continued

mortgagees through whom seller has processed purchaser's application and in the event seller refuses to make said loan to purchaser, purchaser shall have the right to terminate purchaser's contract by _____ days' written

(number)

notice to seller, in which event all sums paid by purchaser to seller, except as hereinafter set forth, shall be returned to purchaser forthwith upon demand, and both seller and purchaser shall be released of all of their respective obligations under this purchase agreement. In case of termination of the agreement, if purchaser has ordered optional or extra items (whether herein specified or hereafter added), all charges for said items or extras shall be immediately due and payable and seller may retain such monies and any monies previously paid on account of such options or extras as liquidated damages, as hereinafter provided.

If purchaser's application is approved by any mortgagee, purchaser promises to execute all forms for payment of mortgages, trust deeds, taxes and hazard insurance and to otherwise comply with all requirements made by lender to complete said loan and to complete said loan on or before the date of closing set forth in the purchase agreement. In the event purchaser fails to complete said loan on or before the closing date, then seller shall have the right, at seller's sole option, to retain all sums paid by purchaser as liquidated damages and seller shall be released from all obligations under the purchase agreement.

SECTION TWO - EXTRAS- Seller and purchaser agree to the following options and/or extras:

<u>Item</u>   <u>Charge</u>

_____   _____

_____   _____

_____   _____

CONTRACT FOR RESIDENCE TO BE ERECTED - Continued

Item   Charge

_____   _____

_____   _____

_____   _____

   Purchaser hereby agrees to pay to seller upon request the total cost of any

personality extras or options and understands that installations of these

personalities or options will not be commenced until payment is received by

seller, unless otherwise specified in writing.

SECTION THREE - CONSTRUCTION OF IMPROVEMENTS- Seller agrees to erect a home on the

property known as Plan No. _____ in substantial

compliance with the plans and specifications therefor and not in conformity with

any model home. Seller shall use its best efforts to complete the improvements on

the above described property on or before _____, 19____,
                                            (month and day)   (yr)

except for delays caused by strikes, acts of God, common enemy, unavailability of

labor, materials and utilities from seller's regular source of supply at prices

acceptable to seller, or other delays beyond the control of seller. Time shall

not be of the essence in reference to completion of construction and the seller

shall not be penalized or liable for damages arising from such delays

aforementioned. If by reason of priorities, allocation of material, or other

regulations of law, seller is unable to obtain construction materials, water or

sewer connections, or other utilities, including but not limited to natural gas,

electricity and telephone, this agreement shall be terminable at the election of

seller upon written notice to purchaser in which event both parties hereto shall

be released from all obligations hereof and the payments made to seller hereunder

shall be returned forthwith to purchaser.

CONTRACT FOR RESIDENCE TO BE ERECTED - Continued

SECTION FOUR - PLANS AND SPECIFICATIONS- Purchaser agrees that the home shall be constructed in substantial compliance with said plans and specifications and not in accordance with any model home, and no additions, modifications, changes and/or alterations to the home requested by purchaser shall be added unless the same is requested in writing by the purchaser and approved by the seller. Any resulting increase in cost due to such additions, modifications, changes or alterations shall be paid by purchaser to seller upon the demand of the seller. The seller shall have the right, but not the obligation, to use any and all sums paid by purchaser hereunder for the construction of the improvements and expenses related thereto.

SECTION FIVE - TITLE INSURANCE- A current commitment for a title insurance policy in an amount equal to the purchase price shall be furnished by seller, at seller's expense, to purchaser at least _____ days prior to closing.
                                   (number)

Subsequent to closing and delivery of deed, seller will cause an owner's title insurance policy in the amount of the purchase price to be issued and delivered to purchaser and shall pay the premium thereon.

SECTION SIX - CONDITION OF TITLE- Title shall be merchantable in seller. Subject to the payment of the purchase price as hereinabove provided and compliance with the other terms and conditions hereof by purchaser, seller shall execute and deliver a good and sufficient warranty deed to purchaser at closing, conveying said property free and clear of all liens and encumbrances except the following, to wit: general taxes for the year of closing and thereafter; easements, rights of way, reservations, restrictive or protective covenants and covenants of record; special assessments whether assessed or not, if any, and subject to any and all building and zoning regulations.

CONTRACT FOR RESIDENCE TO BE ERECTED - Continued

SECTION SEVEN - CLOSING- Closing shall be held on _____,
                                                      (month and day)

19___, or at such earlier date as the parties may agree. The hour and place of
   (yr)

closing shall be designated by mutual agreement. Possession of the property shall

be delivered to purchaser at closing, and delivery of deed.

SECTION EIGHT - OCCUPANCY- Unless otherwise agreed to in writing, the property

shall not be occupied by purchaser until a conveyance therof has been made to

purchaser by seller.

SECTION NINE - PRORATION OF TAXES- General real estate taxes, assessments and

personal property taxes, if any (based on the latest assessment and levy) for the

year in which the conveyance occurs shall be prorated between the seller and

purchaser to the date of closing.

SECTION TEN - ASSIGNMENT- It is further agreed by the parties that this contract

shall not be assigned by purchaser without the prior written consent of seller.

Furthermore, this contract shall not be recorded before consumation of the

transaction covered hereby. If this contract is recorded by purchaser before such

time, seller may elect to void this contract by giving purchaser at least

_____ days' prior written notice thereof, and seller shall have
(number)

the right to retain all payments previously tendered thereunder as liquidated

damages. The recording of this contract shall in no way be construed as imposing

or constituting a cloud upon the title or affecting any sale or conveyance

thereafter. Recordation by seller of a notice of the voiding of this contract

shall constitute a quitclaim deed from purchaser to seller of any and all right,

Page 6 of 10

CONTRACT FOR RESIDENCE TO BE ERECTED - Continued

title and interest purchaser may have had or has in and to the real estate and improvements herein set out. Purchaser specifically appoints seller as purchaser's special attorney-in-fact to accomplish the foregoing acts if seller elects said course of action.

SECTION ELEVEN - INSPECTION OF PREMISES- Purchaser shall not be permitted upon the construction side during working hours on Monday through Friday. Purchaser also agrees that the direction and supervision of the workers on the property, including subcontractors, rests exclusively with seller, and purchaser agrees not to issue any instruction to or otherwise interfere with such workers. Purchaser further agrees not to contract with seller's subcontractors nor to engage other builders or subcontractors except with seller's discretionary consent, and then only in such a manner as will not interfere with seller's completion of the improvements pursuant to this agreement.

SECTION TWELVE - CONDITION OF PREMISES- Seller warrants unto purchaser that the home herein purchased shall be constructed in a good and workmanlike manner. Seller does not, however, warrant against any damage or defects caused by or resulting from the rising or lowering of water tables, expansion or contraction of the soil or other soil conditions. Said warranty shall be for a period of

_____ years from date of completed construction.
(number)

SECTION THIRTEEN - PURCHASER'S REMEDIES- Should seller be unable, or refuse to complete and close the sale of the property by reason of failure of title or because the home shall not be completed as hereinabove provided, then purchaser may demand repayment of the funds previously paid under this agreement, and upon repayment to purchaser of such funds, seller and purchaser shall be relieved of all further obligations hereunder.

CONTRACT FOR RESIDENCE TO BE ERECTED - Continued

SECTION FOURTEEN - PURCHASER'S ACKNOWLEDGEMENT OF DOCUMENTS- Purchaser represents that purchaser has read this contract and that the same constitutes the entire agreement between purchser and seller and no other agreements, promises or warranties except those expressly set forth herein have been made by seller or seller's salespeople, agents and/or servants to purchaser subsequent to execution hereof unless first reduced to writing and executed by the parties hereto.

SECTION FIFTEEN - TIME OF ESSENCE- Time is of the essence hereof, and if any payment or other condition hereof is not made, tendered or performed by either the seller or purchaser as herein provided, then this agreement, at the option of the party who is not in default, may be terminated by such party. In the event of such default by the seller, and the purchaser elects to treat the agreement as terminated, then all payments made hereon shall be returned to the purchaser. In the event of such default by the purchaser and seller elects to treat the agreement as terminated, then all payments made hereunder shall be forfeited and retained by the seller as liquidated damages.

SECTION SIXTEEN - SELLER'S RIGHT TO CURE- If title is not merchantable and written notice of defects is given to the seller within the time herein provided for, delivery of deed and title shall not be rendered merchantable within

_____ days after such written notice, then this contract, at
(number)

purchaser's option, shall be void and of no effect and each party hereto shall be released from all obligations hereunder and the payments made hereunder shall be returned forthwith to purchaser; provided, however, that in lieu of correcting such defects, seller may, within said _____ days, obtain a
(number)

Page 8 of 10

CONTRACT FOR RESIDENCE TO BE ERECTED - Continued

commitment for owner's title insurance policy in the amount of the purchase pice showing the title to be free from such defects and seller shall pay full premium for such title insurance policy.

SECTION SEVENTEEN - APPROVAL- Seller shall have _____ days from
(number)
the execution hereof by purchaser to accept this agreement and upon the acceptance hereof by seller, this agreement shall become a contract between seller and purchaser and all covenants and conditions herein shall be binding on the parties hereto.

SECTION EIGHTEEN - INVALIDITY AND WAIVER- If any term, condition or provision of this agreement is declared illegal or invalid for any reason by a court of competent jurisdiction, the remaining terms, conditions and provisions of this agreement shall, nevertheless, remain in full force and effect. The waiver by the seller of any term, condition or provision of this agreement shall not be construed as a waiver of any other subsequent terms, conditions or provisions of this agreement.

SECTION NINETEEN - CAPTIONS- The captions used herein are merely for easy reference and shall have no effect on the agreement or the terms and conditions herein contained.

SECTION TWENTY - BENEFITS- This agreement shall inure to the benefit of and be binding upon the parties hereto, and their respective successors in interest. Purchaser may not assign this contract or any rights hereunder without the prior written consent of seller.

Page 9 of 10

CONTRACT FOR RESIDENCE TO BE ERECTED - Continued

SECTION TWENTY-ONE - GOVERNING LAW- This agreement shall be construed in accordance with the laws of the State of _____.

SECTION TWENTY-TWO - ADDITIONAL PROVISIONS- _____
(Insert any added provisions or

_____
contingencies not included above)

_____

_____

_____

_____

Upon approval hereof by the seller, this agreement shall become a contract between seller and purchaser and shall inure to the benefit of the heirs, successors and assigns of said parties.

_____   _____
(Purchaser's signature)   (Date)

_____   _____
(Purchaser's signature)   (Date)

The following section is to be completed by seller:

Seller approves the above contract this _____ day of
(number)
_____, 19___ .
(month)   (yr)

_____   _____
(Seller's signature)   (Date)

_____   _____
(Seller's signature   (Date)

EXCHANGE OF PROPERTY

AGREEMENT TO MAKE EXCHANGE OF REAL PROPERTY

Agreement made _____ , 19___ , between:
                    (month and day)   (yr)

_____   and   _____
(Name(s) of first party)   (Name(s) of second party)

herein known as first party, of   herein known as second party, of

_____   _____
(Address)   (Address)

_____   _____
(City)   (City)

_____   _____
(County)   (County)

_____   _____
(State)   (State)

In consideration of their mutual promises set out below, the parties agree as follows:

First party shall sell and convey to second party the property described below as first property free from encumbrances except those set out herein.

Second party shall sell and convey to first party the property described below as second property free from encumbrances except those set out herein.

First property, the property of first party, described as follows:

_____
(Describe property of first party)

_____

_____

EXCHANGE REAL PROPERTY - Continued

will be conveyed to second party: (Cross out Statement A or Statement B)

    A. with no liens and encumbrances.

          OR

    B. subject to the following liens and encumbrances: _____

_____

_____.

    Second property, the property of second party, described as follows:

_____,
(describe property of second party)

_____

_____

will be conveyed to first party: (Cross out Statement A or Statement B)

    A. with no liens and encumbrances.

          OR

    B. subject to the following liens and encumbrances: _____

_____

_____.

    Each conveyance shall be made by means of a _____
                            (quitclaim or warranty or as the

_____ deed conveying the
case may be)

respective properties free of encumbrances, except as herein stated.

    The terms and conditions of such exchange are as follows: _____

_____

_____

EXCHANGE REAL PROPERTY - Continued

_____

_____

_____

_____

_____

_____.

    In witness whereof, the parties have executed this agreement in the City of _____, State of _____, on the day and year first above written.

_____   _____
(Signature of first party)   (Signature of second party)

_____   _____
(Signature of first party)   (Signature of second party)

CONTRACT TO EXCHANGE REAL ESTATE
(With Valuations)

Agreement made _____, 19___, between:
                   (month and day)   (yr)

_____ and _____
(Name(s) of first party)   (Name(s) of second party)

herein known as first party, of   herein known as second party, of

_____   _____
(Address)   (Address)

_____   _____
(City)   (City)

_____   _____
(County)   (County)

_____   _____
(State)   (State)

RECITALS

1. First party agrees to convey to second party the following described real

estate, located at _____
                      (Address)

                      _____
                      (City)

                      _____
                      (County)

                      _____,
                      (State)

and more particularly described as follows: _____
                                       (insert legal description)

_____

_____

with all easements and rights of way appurtaining thereto, all improvements

thereon and all fixtures of a permanent nature, currently on the premises except

Page 1 of 10

EXCHANGE REAL ESTATE (With Valuations) - Continued

(list exceptions)

_____

_____

_____

in their present condition, ordinary wear and tear excepted, and the following

personal property: _____
                        (list any personal property to be included)

_____

_____

_____

_____

by good and sufficient _____ warranty deed (and bill of sale).
                         (type of deed)

Said real (and personal) property, for the purpose of this contract, has a gross

valuation of _____ Dollars ($_____). Said property

will be conveyed subject to the following encumbrances which the second party

_____ assume and agree to pay: _____
(will/will not)   (list encumbrances)

_____

_____

_____

_____.

   If a note and trust deed or mortgage is to be assumed, the second party agrees

to apply for a loan assumption if required and the second party agrees to pay (1)

a loan transfer fee not to exceed _____ Dollars ($_____)

and (2) an interest rate not to exceed _____ per cent (%_____)

per annum. If the lender's consent to a loan assumption is required, this contract

Page 2 of 10

EXCHANGE REAL ESTATE (With Valuations) - Continued

is expressly conditioned upon obtaining such consent without change in the terms and conditions of such loan except as above stated.

If a secured or unsecured loan is to be carried by the first party, first party shall not be obligated to carry said loan for any person or entity in lieu of the second party named herein.

Cost of any appraisal for loan purposes to be obtained after this date shall be paid by _____.
(first party/second party/ or as the case may be)

2. Second party agrees to convey to first party the following described real estate, located at

_____
(Address)

_____
(City)

_____
(County)

_____
(State)

and more particularly described as follows: _____
(insert legal description)

_____

_____

with all easements and rights of way appurtaining thereto, all improvements thereon and all fixtures of a permanent nature, currently on the premises except

_____
(list exceptions)

_____

in their present condition, ordinary wear and tear excepted, and the following personal property: _____
(list any personal property to be included)

Page 3 of 10

EXCHANGE REAL ESTATE (With Valuations) - Continued

_____

_____

_____

_____

_____

_____

by good and sufficient _____ warranty deed (and bill of sale).
(type of deed)

Said real (and personal) property, for the purpose of this contract, has a gross

valuation of _____ Dollars ($_____). Said property

will be conveyed subject to the following encumbrances which the first party

_____ assume and agree to pay: _____
(will/will not)   (list encumbrances)

_____

_____

_____.

    If a note and trust deed or mortgage is to be assumed, the first party agrees
to apply for a loan assumption if required and the first party agrees to pay (1)
a loan transfer fee not to exceed _____ Dollars ($_____)
and (2) an interest rate not to exceed _____ per cent (%_____)
per annum. If the lender's consent to a loan assumption is required, this contract
is expressly conditioned upon obtaining such consent without change in the terms
and conditions of such loan except as above stated.

    If a secured or unsecured loan is to be carried by the second party, second party
shall not be obligated to carry said loan for any person or entity in lieu of the
first party named herein.

EXCHANGE REAL ESTATE (With Valuations) - Continued

Cost of any appraisal for loan purposes to be obtained after this date shall be paid by _____.
(first party/second party/ or as the case may be)

SECTION ONE - DIFFERENCE BETWEEN VALUES OF PROPERTIES- The difference between the values of the respective properties, after having considered and deducted the encumbrances above described, shall be deemed for the purposes of this agreement to be _____ Dollars ($_____) and said sum shall be due and payable by _____ party to _____ party
(first/second)   (first/second) as follows:

_____
(describe method of payment)

_____.

SECTION TWO - TITLE- Title shall be merchantable in the respective parties hereto. Each party agrees, at each party's option and expense, to furnish to the other party, on or before _____, 19___, an abstract of title
(month and day)   (yr)
to that party's property, certified to date, or a current commitment for title insurance policy. If either party elects to furnish said title insurance commitment, that party will deliver the title insurance policy to the other party after closing and pay the premium thereon. Except as stated in paragraphs 1 and 2, if title is not merchantable and written notice of defect(s) is given by either party to the other party within the time herein provided for delivery of deed and shall not be rendered merchantable within _____ days of such
(number)
written notice, then this contract, at the option of the party giving such notice, shall be void and of no effect and each party hereto shall be released from all obligations hereunder; provided, however, that in lieu of correcting such defect(s), the party receiving such notice may, within said _____
(number)

Page 5 of 10

EXCHANGE REAL ESTATE (With Valuations) - Continued

days, obtain a committment for owner's title insurance policy in the amount or the purchase price reflecting title insurance protection in regard to such defect(s), and the party giving such notice shall have the option of accepting the then existing insured title in lieu of such merchantable title. The party receiving such notice shall pay the full premium for such owner's title insurance policy, and the abstract, if any, shall be returned by the other party.

SECTION THREE - PRORATION OF TAXES- General taxes for the year of closing shall be apportioned to dates of delivery of deeds based on the most recent levy and the most recent assessment. Personal property taxes, prepaid rents, water rents, sewer rents, FHA mortgage insurance premiums, interest on encumbrances, if any, and

_____
(list loans remaining on each property)

_____

_____

shall be apportioned to date of delivery of deed with respect to each property. Each party shall give credit at closing for any tenant security deposits. Loan balances are to be adjusted at the time of closing. Any encumbrances required to be paid may be paid at the time of settlement from the proceeds of this transaction or from any other source.

SECTION FOUR - EXECUTION AND DELIVERY OF DEEDS- Each party agrees to execute and deliver that party's deed to the other party on _____, 19____,
                                                   (month and day)   (yr)

or, by mutual agreement, at an earlier date, conveying that party's property free and clear of all taxes (including special improvements now installed, whether assessed or not unless specifically hereinafter excepted), except general taxes for the year of closing which other party assumes and agrees to pay subject to the

EXCHANGE REAL ESTATE (With Valuations) - Continued

adjustment herein provided for. The property of each party shall be subject to building and zoning regulations pertaining thereto and shall be subject to any tenancies hereinafter set forth and shall be free and clear of all leins and encumbrances except those hereinabove described, and except:

As to the property described in paragraph 1, insert any reservations, restrictive covenants, easements, right of way, special taxes or any other exceptions to which property is subject (if none, insert "none"):

_____

_____

_____

_____

_____

_____

_____ .

As to the property described in paragraph 2, insert any reservations, restrictive covenants, easements, right of way, special taxes or any other exceptions to which property is subject (if none, insert "none"):

_____

_____

_____

_____

_____

_____ .

EXCHANGE REAL ESTATE (With Valuations) - Continued

SECTION FIVE - CLOSING- The hour and place of closing shall be designated by mutual consent.

SECTION SIX - POSSESSION- Possession of the premises shall be delivered to each purchaser concurrently with the transfer of title or as follows:

_____

_____.

The property described in paragraph 1 shall be subject to the following leases or tenancies: _____

_____

_____

_____,

and the property described in paragraph 2 shall be subject to the following leases or tenancies: _____

_____

_____

_____.

SECTION SEVEN - DESTRUCTION OF PREMISES- In the event that either of the properties is damaged by fire or other casualty prior to the time of closing in an amount of not more than ten percent of the value of the property, the seller of said damaged property shall be obligated to repair the same before the date herein provided for delivery of deed. In the event such damage cannot be repaired within said time or if damage shall exceed such value, this contract may be cancelled at the option of the other party. Should the other party elect to carry out this

EXCHANGE REAL ESTATE (With Valuations) - Continued

agreement despite such damage, such other party shall be entitled to all the credit for the insurance proceeds resulting from such damage not exceeding, however, the total value. Should any fixtures or services fail between the date of this agreement and the date of possession or the date of delivery of deed, whichever shall be earlier, then the owner of such property shall be responsible for the repair or replacement of such fixtures or services with a unit of similar size, age and quality, or an equivalent credit.

SECTION EIGHT - EXAMINATION OF PREMISES-   Both parties have examined the properties and accept the same in the present condition. Neither party is relying on representations of the other party as to zoning other than as specifically set forth herein.

SECTION NINE - GOOD FAITH- First party herewith deposits in trust account at
_____ bank for the second party the sum of
_____ Dollars ($_____) by _____
(amount of earnest money)   (cash/check/note)
and second party herewith deposits in said trust account for first party the sum
of _____ Dollars ($_____) by _____,
(amount of earnest money)   (cash/check/note)
as a guaranty of good faith, to be returned to the respective parties when the transaction is completed.

SECTION TEN - TIME OF THE ESSENCE- Time is of the essence hereof, and if any payment or other condition hereof is not made, tendered or performed by either of the parties hereto as herein provided, then this contract, at the option of the party who is not in default may be terminated. In case of such termination, the

EXCHANGE REAL ESTATE (With Valuations) - Continued

earnest money held in a trust account with _____ shall

                                 (name of bank)

be given to the non-defaulting party.

SECTION ELEVEN - BINDING EFFECT- This contract shall be binding upon and shall inure to the benefit of the parties hereto, their heirs, successors and assigns.

SECTION TWELVE - CAPTIONS- The captions used herein are merely for easy reference and shall have no effect on the agreement or on the terms and conditions herein contained.

SECTION THIRTEEN - ADDITIONAL PROVISIONS- Additional provisions, if any:

_____

_____

_____

_____

_____

_____

_____.

In the event this instrument is not signed by all parties hereto on or before

_____, 19____, this agreement shall become void and of no

(month and day)   (yr)

effect.

IN WITNESS WHEREOF the parties hereto have set their hands and seals the day and year first above written.

_____   _____
(Signature of first party)   (Signature of second party)

_____   _____
(Signature of first party)   (Signature of second party)

CONTRACT TO EXCHANGE REAL ESTATE
(Without Valuations)

Agreement made _____, 19____, between:
               (month and day)   (yr)

_____ and _____
(Name(s) of first party)   (Name(s) of second party)

herein known as first party, of   herein known as second party, of

_____   _____
(Address)   (Address)

_____   _____
(City)   (City)

_____   _____
(County)   (County)

_____   _____
(State)   (State)

RECITALS

1. First party agrees to convey to second party the following described real

estate, located at _____
                     (Address)

                    _____
                     (City)

                    _____
                     (County)

                    _____
                     (State)

and more particularly described as follows: _____
                                     (insert legal description)

_____

_____

with all easements and rights of way appurtaining thereto, all improvements

thereon and all fixtures of a permanent nature, currently on the premises except

Page 1 of 10

EXCHANGE REAL ESTATE (Without Valuations) - Continued

(list exceptions) _____

_____

in their present condition, ordinary wear and tear excepted, and the following

personal property: _____
(list any personal property to be included)

_____

_____

_____

_____

_____

by good and sufficient _____ warranty deed (and bill of sale).
(type of deed)

Said property will be conveyed subject to the following encumbrances which the

second party _____ assume and agree to pay: _____
(will/will not)   (list encumbrances)

_____

_____

_____

_____.

If a note and trust deed or mortgage is to be assumed, the second party agrees

to apply for a loan assumption if required and the second party agrees to pay (1)

a loan transfer fee not to exceed _____ Dollars ($_____)

and (2) an interest rate not to exceed _____ per cent (%_____)

per annum. If the lender's consent to a loan assumption is required, this contract

is expressly conditioned upon obtaining such consent without change in the terms

and conditions of such loan except as above stated.

EXCHANGE REAL ESTATE (Without Valuations) - Continued

If a secured or unsecured loan is to be carried by the first party, first party shall not be obligated to carry said loan for any person or entity in lieu of the second party named herein.

Cost of any appraisal for loan purposes to be obtained after this date shall be paid by _____.

(first party/second party/or as the case may be)

2. Second party agrees to convey to first party the following described real estate, located at _____

(Address)

_____

(City)

_____

(County)

_____

(State)

and more particularly described as follows: _____

(insert legal description)

_____

_____

with all easements and rights of way appurtaining thereto, all improvements thereon and all fixtures of a permanent nature, currently on the premises except

_____

(list exceptions)

_____

in their present condition, ordinary wear and tear excepted, and the following personal property: _____

(list any personal property to be included)

_____

Page 3 of 10

EXCHANGE REAL ESTATE (Without Valuations) - Continued

_____

_____

_____

_____

by good and sufficient _____ warranty deed (and bill of sale).
                           (type of deed)

Said property will be conveyed subject to the following encumbrances which the

first party _____ assume and agree to pay: _____
            (will/will not)   (list encumbrances)

_____

_____

_____

_____.

If a note and trust deed or mortgage is to be assumed, the first party agrees to

apply for a loan assumption if required and the first party agrees to pay (1) a

loan transfer fee not to exceed _____ Dollars ($_____)

and (2) an interest rate not to exceed _____ per cent (%_____)

per annum. If the lender's consent to a loan assumption is required, this contract

is expressly conditioned upon obtaining such consent without change in the terms

and conditions of such loan except as above stated.

If a secured or unsecured loan is to be carried by the second party, second

party shall not be obligated to carry said loan for any person or entity in lieu

of the first party named herein.

Cost of any appraisal for loan purposes to be obtained after this date shall be

paid by _____.
        (first party/second party/ or as the case may be)

EXCHANGE REAL ESTATE (Without Valuations) - Continued

SECTION ONE - DIFFERENCE BETWEEN VALUES OF PROPERTIES- The difference between the values of the respective properties, after having considered and deducted the encumbrances above described, shall be deemed for the purposes of this agreement to be _____ Dollars ($_____) and said sum shall be due and payable by _____ party to _____ party
_____(first/second)_____   _____(first/second)_____

as follows: _____
       (describe method of payment)

_____.

SECTION TWO - TITLE- Title shall be merchantable in the respective parties hereto. Each party agrees, at each party's option and expense, to furnish to the other party, on or before _____, 19___, an abstract of title
               (month and day)   (yr)

to that party's property, certified to date, or a current commitment for title insurance policy. If either party elects to furnish said title insurance committment, that party will deliver the title insurance policy to the other party after closing and pay the premium thereon. Except as stated in paragraphs 1 and 2, if title is not merchantable and written notice of defect(s) is given by either party to the other party within the time herein provided for delivery of deed and shall not be rendered merchantable within _____ days of such
               (number)

written notice, then this contract, at the option of the party giving such notice, shall be void and of no effect and each party hereto shall be released from all obligations hereunder; provided, however, that in lieu of correcting such defect(s), the party receiving such notice may, within said _____
               (number)

days, obtain a commitment for owner's title insurance policy in the amount or the purchase price reflecting title insurance protection in regard to such defect(s),

EXCHANGE REAL ESTATE (Without Valuations) - Continued

and the party giving such notice shall have the option of accepting the then existing insured title in lieu of such merchantable title. The party receiving such notice shall pay the full premium for such owner's title insurance policy, and the abstract, if any, shall be returned by the other party.

SECTION THREE - PRORATION OF TAXES- General taxes for the year of closing shall be apportioned to dates of delivery of deeds based on the most recent levy and the most recent assessment. Personal property taxes, prepaid rents, water rents, sewer rents, FHA mortgage insurance premiums, interest on encumbrances, if any, and

_____
(list loans remaining on each property)

_____

_____

shall be apportioned to date of delivery of deed with respect to each property. Each party shall give credit at closing for any tenant security deposits. Loan balances are to be adjusted at the time of closing. Any encumbrances required to be paid may be paid at the time of settlement from the proceeds of this transaction or from any other source.

SECTION FOUR - EXECUTION AND DELIVERY OF DEEDS- Each party agrees to execute and deliver that party's deed to the other party on _____, 19____,
                                                                              (month and day)   (yr)
or, by mutual agreement, at an earlier date, conveying that party's property free and clear of all taxes (including special improvements now installed, whether assessed or not unless specifically hereinafter excepted), except general taxes for the year of closing which said other party assumes and agrees to pay subject to the adjustment herein provided for. The property of each party shall be

EXCHANGE REAL ESTATE (Without Valuations) - Continued

subject to building and zoning regulations pertaining thereto and shall be subject to any tenancies hereinafter set forth and shall be free and clear of all leins and encumbrances except those hereinabove described, and except:

As to the property described in paragraph 1, insert any reservations, restrictive covenants, easements, right of way, special taxes or any other exceptions to which property is subject (if none, insert "none"):

_____

_____

_____

_____

_____

_____.

As to the property described in paragraph 2, insert any reservations, restrictive covenants, easements, right of way, special taxes or any other exceptions to which property is subject (if none, insert "none"):

_____

_____

_____

_____

_____

_____.

EXCHANGE REAL ESTATE (Without Valuations) - Continued

SECTION FIVE - CLOSING- The hour and place of closing shall be designated by mutual consent.

SECTION SIX - POSSESSION- Possession of the premises shall be delivered to each purchaser concurrently with the transfer of title or as follows: _____

_____

_____.

The property described in paragraph 1 shall be subject to the following leases or tenancies: _____

_____

_____

_____,

and the property described in paragraph 2 shall be subject to the following leases or tenancies: _____

_____

_____

_____.

SECTION SEVEN - DESTRUCTION OF PREMISES- In the event that either of the properties is damaged by fire or other casualty prior to the time of closing in an amount of not more than ten percent of the value of the property, the seller of said damaged property shall be obligated to repair the same before the date herein provided for delivery of deed. In the event such damage cannot be repaired within said time or if damage shall exceed such value, this contract may be cancelled at the option of the other party. Should the other party elect to carry out this agreement despite such damage, such other party shall be entitled to all the

EXCHANGE REAL ESTATE (Without Valuations) - Continued

credit for the insurance proceeds resulting from such damage not exceeding,
however, the total value. Should any fixtures or services fail between the date
of this agreement and the date of possession or the date of delivery of deed,
whichever shall be earlier, then the owner of such property shall be responsible
for the repair or replacement of such fixtures or services with a unit of similar
size, age and quality, or an equivalent credit.

SECTION EIGHT - EXAMINATION OF PREMISES- Both parties have examined the
properties and accept the same in the present condition. Neither party is relying
on representations of the other party as to zoning other than as specifically set
forth herein.

SECTION NINE - GOOD FAITH- First party herewith deposits in trust account at
_____ bank for the second party the sum of _____
(name of bank)
Dollars ($_____) by _____ and second party
                          (cash/check/note)
herewith deposits in trust account for first party in said trust account the sum
of _____ Dollars ($_____) by _____,
                                                   (cash/check/note)
as a guaranty of good faith, to be returned to the respective parties when the
transaction is completed.

SECTION TEN - TIME OF THE ESSENCE- Time is of the essence hereof, and if any
payment or other condition hereof is not made, tendered or performed by either of
the parties hereto as herein provided, then this contract, at the option of the
party who is not in default may be terminated. In case of such termination, the
earnest money held in a trust account with _____ shall
                                           (name of bank)
be given to the non-defaulting party.

EXCHANGE REAL ESTATE (Without Valuations) - Continued

SECTION ELEVEN - BINDING EFFECT- This contract shall be binding upon and shall inure to the benefit of the parties hereto, their heirs, successors and assigns.

SECTION TWELVE - CAPTIONS- The captions used herein are merely for easy reference and shall have no effect on the agreement or on the terms and conditions herein contained.

SECTION THIRTEEN - ADDITIONAL PROVISIONS- Additional provisions, if any:

_____

_____

_____

_____

_____

_____

_____.

In the event this instrument is not signed by all parties hereto on or before

_____, 19____, this agreement shall become void and of no
(month and day)   (yr)

effect.

IN WITNESS WHEREOF the parties hereto have set their hands and seals the day and year first above written.

_____   _____
(signature of first party)   (signature of second party)

_____   _____
(signature of first party)   (signature of second party)

POWER OF ATTORNEY

GENERAL POWER OF ATTORNEY

State of _____

County of _____ ss:

Know all men by these presents, that I, _____, the
                                                        (name)

undersigned of:

_____
(Address)

_____
(City)

_____
(County)

_____
(State)

do hereby make, constitute, and appoint _____ of:
                                                     (name)

_____
(Address)

_____
(City)

_____
(County)

_____
(State)

my true and lawful attorney-in-fact for me and in my name, place, and stead, and
on my behalf, and for my use and benefit:

1. To exercise or perform any act, power, duty, right, or obligation whatsoever
that I now have, or may hereafter acquire the legal right, power, or capacity to
exercise or perform, in connection with, arising from, or relating to any person,
item, transaction, thing, business property, real or personal, tangible or
intangible, or matter whatsoever;

GENERAL POWER OF ATTORNEY - Continued

2. To request, ask, demand, sue for, recover, collect, receive, and hold and possess all such sums of money, debts, dues, commercial paper, checks, drafts, accounts, deposits, legacies, bequests, devises, notes, interests, stock certificates, bonds, dividends, certificates of deposit, annuities, pension and retirement benefits, insurance benefits and proceeds, any and all documents of title, choses in action, personal and real property, intangible and tangible property and property rights, and demands whatsoever, liquidated or unliquidated, as now are, or shall hereafter become, owned by, or due, owing, payable, or belonging to, me or in which I have or may hereafter acquire interest, to have, use, and take all lawful means and equitable and legal remedies, procedures, and writs in my name for the collection and recovery thereof, and to adjust, sell, compromise, and agree for the same, and to make, execute, and deliver for me, on my behalf, and in my name, all endorsements, acquittances, releases, receipts, or other sufficient discharges for the same;

3. To lease, purchase, exchange, and acquire, and to agree, bargain, and contract for the lease, purchase, exchange, and acquisition of, and to accept, take, receive, and possess any real or personal property whatsoever, tangible or intangible, or interest thereon, on such terms and conditions, and under such covenants, as said attorney-in-fact shall deem proper;

4. To maintain, repair, improve, manage, insure, rent, lease, sell, convey, subject to liens, mortgage, subject to deed of trust, and hypothecate, and in any way or manner deal with all or any part of any real or personal property whatsoever, tangible or intangible, or any interest therein, that I now own or may hereafter acquire, for me, in my behalf, and in my name and under such terms and conditions, and under such covenants, as said attorney-in-fact shall deem proper;

Page 2 of 4

GENERAL POWER OF ATTORNEY - Continued

5. To conduct, engage in, and transact any and all lawful business of whatever nature of kind for me, on my behalf, and in my name;

6. To make, receive, sign, endorse, execute, acknowledge, deliver, and possess such applications, contracts, agreements, options, covenants, conveyances, deeds, trust deeds, security agreements, bills of sale, leases, mortgages, assignments, insurance policies, bills of lading, warehouse receipts, documents of title, bills, bonds, debentures, checks, drafts, bills of exchange, letters of credit, notes, stock certificates, proxies, warrants, commercial paper, receipts, withdrawal receipts and deposit instruments relating to accounts or deposits in, or certificates of deposit of, banks, savings and loan or other institutions or associations, proofs of loss, evidences of debts, releases, and satisfaction of mortgages, liens, judgments, security agreements and other debts and obligations and such other instruments in writing of whatever kind and nature as may be necessary or proper in the exercise of the rights and powers herein granted.

7. I grant to said attorney-in-fact full power and authority to do, take, and perform all and every act and thing whatsoever requisite, proper, or necessary to be done, in the exercise of any of the rights and powers herein granted, as fully to all intents and purposes as I might or could do if personally present, with full power of substitution or revocation, hereby ratifying and confirming all that said attorney-in-fact, or _____ substitute or substitutes, shall
(his or her)
lawfully do or cause to be done by virtue of this power of attorney and the rights and powers herein granted.

8. This instrument is to be construed and interpreted as a general power of attorney. The enumeration of specific items, rights, acts, or powers herein is not intended to, nor does it, limit or restrict, and is not to be construed or

GENERAL POWER OF ATTORNEY - Continued

interpreted as limiting or restricting, the general powers herein granted to said attorney-in-fact.

9. The rights, powers, and authority of said attorney-in-fact herein granted shall commence and be in full force and effect on _____, 19 ___,
                                                                                    (month and day)   (yr)

and such rights, powers, and authority shall remain in full force and effect thereafter until _____
                                   (set forth specific period of time, date of termination,

_____.
contingency on which power terminates, or method of termination, such as by

_____.
written notice.)

    Dated _____, 19 ___.
                        (month and day)   (yr)

                                 _____
                                 (Signature)

CERTIFICATE OF NOTARY

State of _____)
                                       ss:

County of _____)

    On this _____ day of _____, in the year 19 ___, before me personally came and appeared _____, known, and known to me, to be the individual described in and who executed the foregoing instrument, and who duly acknowledged to me that he/she executed same for the purpose therein contained.

    In witness whereof, I hereunto set my hand and official seal.

                                 _____
                                 (Notary Public)

                                 My commission expires: _____.

POWER OF ATTORNEY: SPECIFIC CONDITIONS

KNOW MEN BY ALL THESE PRESENTS: That

_____ of
(Name of owner)

_____
(Address)

_____
(City)

_____
(County)

_____
(State)

reposing special trust and confidence in

_____ of
(Name of appointee)

_____
(Address)

_____
(City)

_____
(County)

_____,
(State)

has made, constituted and appointed, and by these presents does make,

constitute and appoint the said _____ true and lawful
(name of appointee)

attorney for _____ and in _____ name, place and stead, to
(me/us)   (my/our)

accomplish the sale, pledging, mortgaging, negotiation, or any contemplated

act with regard to the following described property to wit:

_____
(legal description of property)

_____

_____,

Page 1 of 3

POWER OF ATTORNEY: SPECIFIC CONDITIONS - Continued

also known and numbered as:

_____
(Property address)

_____
(City)

_____
(County)

_____.
(State)

Hereby giving and granting unto said attorney full power and authority to negotiate, do and perform all and every act and thing whatsoever requisite and necessary to be done in and about the premises, as fully to all intent and purposes as _____ might do if personally present, including, but not
            (I/we)

limited to, the execution of deeds conveying real estate, with full power to sell and convey, and the execution of mortgages and deeds of trust and any and all documents related to any transfer or encumbrance, including closing and settlement sheets in connection with said transfer or encumbrance; with full power of revocation hereby ratifying and confirming that said attorney shall lawfully do or cause to be done by virtue hereof.

This power of attorney shall not be affected by disability of the principal.

IN WITNESS WHEREOF, _____ have hereunto set _____ hand and seal
                (I/we)   (my/our)

this _____ day of _____, 19____.
   (number of date)   (month)   (yr)

_____
(Name signed and printed)

_____

_____
(Name signed and printed)

_____

POWER OF ATTORNEY: SPECIFIC CONDITIONS - Continued

STATE OF _____

COUNTY OF _____

The foregoing instrument was acknowledged before me this _____

day of _____ , 19____ by _____

_____ .

Witness my hand and official seal.

My commission expires: _____ .

                                    _____
                                    NOTARY PUBLIC

REVOCATION OF POWER OF ATTORNEY

State of _____)

)   ss:

County of _____)

KNOW YE ALL MEN BY THESE PRESENTS,

That I, _____, of:

    (name)

        _____
        (Address)

        _____
        (City)

        _____
        (County)

        _____
        (State)

in and by a letter of attorney dated the _____ day of _____,

                                 (number)   (month)

19 ____, did make, constitute and appoint _____, of:

 (yr)   (name)

        _____
        (Address)

        _____
        (City)

        _____
        (County)

        _____
        (State)

by said letter of attorney as my attorney-in-fact.

REVOCATION OF POWER OF ATTORNEY - Continued

BY THESE PRESENTS, I do hereby revoke, countermand and make null and void the aforesaid letter of attorney, and all right, power and authority thereby given, or intended to be given, to the aforesaid _____.

(name of attorney-in-fact)

IN WITNESS WHEREOF, I have hereunto set my hand and seal this _____ day

(number)

of _____, 19 ____.

(month)   (yr)

_____

(Signature)

CERTIFICATE OF NOTARY

State of _____)

)   ss

County of _____)

On this _____ day of _____, in the year 19 ____, before me personally came and appeared _____, known, and known to me, to be the individual described in and who executed the foregoing instrument, and who duly acknowledged to me that he/she executed same for the purpose therein contained.

In witness whereof, I hereunto set my hand and official seal.

_____

(Notary Public)

My commission expires: _____.

Page 2 of 2

PROMISSORY NOTES

EARNEST MONEY PROMISSORY NOTE

Date of making _____, 19____,
                (month and day)   (yr)

Place of making
                        _____
                        (Address)

                        _____
                        (City)

                        _____
                        (County)

                        _____
                        (State)

                                        and

_____   _____
(Name(s) of purchaser)   (Name(s) of lender)

herein known as purchaser, of   herein known as lender, of

_____   _____
(Address)   (Address)

_____   _____
(City)   (City)

_____   _____
(County)   (County)

_____   _____
(State)   (State)

$_____
 (Amount of earnest money taken in form of a note)

FOR VALUE RECEIVED, _____, jointly and
                         (name(s) of prospective purchaser)

severally, promise to pay to the order of _____ the
                                           (name of lender)

sum of _____ Dollars ($_____), together with

interest at the rate of _____ per cent (_____%) per annum

from _____ until paid.
      (due date)

Page 1 of 2

EARNEST MONEY PROMISSORY NOTE - Continued

Both principal and interest are payable in U.S. dollars on or before

_____, 19____, payable at
(month and day)   (yr)

_____
(Address)

_____
(City)

_____
(County)

_____
(State)

or at any such other address as note holder may designate. Presentment, notice of dishonor, and protest are hereby waived. If this note is not paid when due,

_____ agree to pay, all reasonable costs of collection, including attorneys'
(I/we)

fees.

_____
(Signature of purchaser)

_____
(Signature of purchaser)

This note is given as earnest money for the contract on the following property

_____
(Address)

_____
(City)

_____
(County)

_____
(State)

for an offer dated _____, 19___, tendered to sellers by
(month and day)   (yr)

_____ as purchasers.
(name(s) of purchaser)

Page 2 of 2

INSTALLMENT NOTE

Agreement made _____, 19 ____, between:
　　　　　　　　　(month and day)　　　　　　　(yr)

_____　　　　_____
(Name of maker)　　　　　　　　　(Name of lender)

herein known as maker, of　　　　herein known as lender, of

_____　　　　_____
(Address)　　　　　　　　　　　　(Address)

_____　　　　_____
(City)　　　　　　　　　　　　　　(City)

_____　　　　_____
(County)　　　　　　　　　　　　　(County)

_____　　　　_____
(State)　　　　　　　　　　　　　(State)

$ _____
(Amount of loan)

I promise to pay the sum of _____ Dollars

($_____) to the order of _____ in the
　　　　　　　　　　　　　　　(name of lender)

following manner:

The sum of _____ Dollars ($_____) on the

_____ day of _____, 19 ____; and the sum of
(number)　　　　　　(month)　　　　　(yr)

_____ Dollars ($_____) on the _____
　　　　　　　　　　　　　　　　　　　　　　　　　　　　　(number)

of each month thereafter until the entire amount is repaid, together with interest

at the rate of _____ (_____%) percent per annum,

payable with each installment of the principal.

Page 1 of 2

INSTALLMENT NOTE - Continued

The maker and endorser of this note further agree to waive demand, notice of nonpayment and protest, and in case suit shall be brought for the collection hereof, or the same has to be collected upon demand of an attorney, to pay reasonable attorney's fees for making such collection. Deferred interest payments to bear interest from maturity at _____ (_____%) percent per annum, payable semiannually.

_____
(Signature of maker)

_____
(Signature of endorser)

PROMISSORY NOTE

Agreement made _____, 19 ____, between:
          (month and day)   (yr)

_____
(Name of maker)

herein known as maker, of

_____
(Address)

_____
(City)

_____
(County)

_____
(State)

_____
(Name of lender)

herein known as lender, of

_____
(Address)

_____
(City)

_____
(County)

_____
(State)

$_____
(Amount of loan)

_____ days after the above date I promise to pay to the order of
(Number)

_____, the sum of _____
(name of lender)

_____Dollars ($_____), together with

interest at _____ (_____%) percent per annum.

    The maker and endorser of this note further agree to waive demand, notice of nonpayment and protest, and in case suit shall be brought for the collection hereof, or the same has to be collected upon demand of an attorney, to pay reasonable attorney's fees for making such collection. Deferred interest payments to bear interest from maturity at _____ (_____%) percent per annum, payable semiannually.

_____
(Signature of endorser)

_____
(Signature of maker)

Due _____, 19 ____
     (month and day)   (yr)

PROMISSORY NOTE: PAYABLE ON DEMAND

Agreement made _____, 19____, between:
           (month and day)   (yr)

_____   and   _____
(Name of maker)   (Name of lender)

herein referred to as maker, of   herein referred to as lender, of

_____   _____
(Address)   (Address)

_____   _____
(City)   (City)

_____   _____
(County)   (County)

_____   _____
(State)   (State)

$ _____
   (Amount of loan)

For value received, I promise to pay to the order of _____
                                                       (name of lender)

_____, payable on demand the sum of

_____ Dollars ($_____), with interest at the

rate of _____ percent (_____%) per annum thereon from

_____, 19 ____, in the form of _____
(month and day)   (yr)   (cash, check, cashier's check or

_____.
money order)

In case of more than one borrower, each borrower agrees to be jointly and
severally liable for all amounts payable under this note.

If action is instituted on this note, the prevailing party shall be entitled to
reasonable attorneys' fees and costs.

_____
(Signature of maker)

Page 1 of 1

RESIDENTIAL LEASES

AGREEMENT TO LEASE RESIDENTIAL PROPERTY

Agreement made _____, 19____, between:
(month and day)   (yr)

_____   and   _____
(Name(s) of landlord)   (Name(s) of tenant

herein known as   herein known as
prospective landlord, of   prospective tenant, of

_____   _____
(Address)   (Address)

_____   _____
(City)   (City)

_____   _____
(County)   (County)

_____   _____
(State)   (State)

RECITALS -

1. Prospective landlord is the owner of real property that will shortly be available for lease.

2. Prospective landlord desires to lease residential property for prospective tenant's personal use.

3. The parties desire to establish an agreement to insure a future lease of the residential property described herein.

In consideration of the mutual covenants contained herein, the parties agree as follows:

SECTIONONE- SUBJECT OF LEASE - Prospective landlord shall enter intoawritten lease agreement with prospective tenant on or before _____, 19 ____, (month and day)   (yr)

whereby prospective landlord shall lease to prospective tenant the residential

Page 1 of 4

LEASE OF RESIDENTIAL PROPERTY - Continued

property owned by prospective landlord located at:

_____
(Address)

_____
(City)

_____
(County)

_____
(State)

for prospective tenant and _____ family to occupy and use as their
                                 (his or her)
residence.

SECTION TWO - TERM OF LEASE - The premises shall be leased to prospective tenant

for a period of _____ years from _____, 19 ____, and
                    (number)   (month and day)   (yr)

prospective tenant shall have the option to renew the lease for _____
                                                                    (number)

additional periods of equal duration, on giving _____ days' written
                                                    (number)

notice to prospective landlord of _____ intent to exercise that option at
                                    (his/her/their)

least _____ days prior to the expiration of the lease. Thereafter any
         (number)

additional extensions of the initial lease agreement or any new lease agreement

shall be at the option of prospective landlord.

SECTION THREE - MONTHLY RENTAL - Prospective tenant shall pay

_____ Dollars ($_____) per month as monthly

rental for the term of the lease with the first payment due on or before

_____, 19 ____, and subsequent payments on the _____
(month and day)   (yr)   (number)

Page 2 of 4

LEASE OF RESIDENTIAL PROPERTY - Continued

day of each succeeding month. This rental payment shall be subject to renegotiation by the parties at any time either of the parties exercises that party's option to renew the lease under the provisions of any subsequent lease agreement.

SECTION FOUR - TAXES AND UTILITIES - Prospective landlord shall be liablefor the payment of all real property taxes assessed against the residential premises and shall pay the costs incurred for _____
(list services landlord will pay for)

_____.

Prospective tenant shall be liable for payment of all utilities and services, except: _____
(list any exceptions)

_____.

SECTION FIVE - REPAIRS - Prospective tenant shall make all repairs on the premises, except where repairs are necessitated by structural damage, after advising prospective landlord of the necessity therefor. Prospective landlord shall reimburse prospective tenant for the costs of all material required by the repairs made by prospective tenant. Prospective landlord shall be responsible for making all structural repairs at landlord's own expense.

SECTION SIX - LIQUIDATED DAMAGES - Prospective tenant shall pay prospective landlord _____ Dollars ($_____) as liquidated damages for the refusal or failure by prospective tenant to execute a subsequent lease agreement in accordance with the terms herein. The parties acknowledge that a failure to execute that lease will result in damages being suffered by prospective landlord, the extent of which cannot be estimated or determined.

Page 3 of 4

LEASE OF RESIDENTIAL PROPERTY - Continued

In witness whereof, the parties have executed this agreement in the City of

_____, State of _____,

the day and year first above written.

_____   _____
(Signature of prospective landlord)   (Signature of prospective tenant)

_____   _____
(Signature of prospective landlord)   (Signature of prospective tenant)

EXTENSION OF LEASE

Agreement made _____, 19____, between:
　　　　　　　　(month and day)　　　　　　　(yr)

_____　and　_____
(Name(s) of landlord)　　　　　　　　(Name(s) of tenant)

herein known as landlord, of　　　herein known as tenant, of

_____　　　　_____
(Address)　　　　　　　　　　　　(Address)

_____　　　　_____
(City)　　　　　　　　　　　　　(City)

_____　　　　_____
(County)　　　　　　　　　　　　(County)

_____　　　　_____
(State)　　　　　　　　　　　　(State)

Date lease was signed: _____, 19 ____.
　　　　　　　　　　　　(month and day)　　　　　(yr)

　　Beginning: _____, 19 ____.
　　　　　　　(month and day)　　　　　(yr)

　　Ending: _____, 19 ____.
　　　　　　(month and day)　　　　　(yr)

1. The above-described lease, due to expire on _____,
　　　　　　　　　　　　　　　　　　　　　(month and day)

19 ____, is hereby renewed for a term of _____ beginning
(yr)　　　　　　　　　　　　　　　(amount of time)

_____, 19 ____ and ending _____,
(month and day)　　　　(yr)　　　　　　　(month and day)

19 ____.
(yr)

2. All terms, provisions and covenants of the above-described lease shall remain in full force for the duration of the extended term, except as noted.

Page 1 of 2

EXTENSION OF LEASE - Continued

3.   In connection with this renewal, the rent, payable monthly, shall be

_____ Dollars ($ _____) per month, making

a total rental of _____ Dollars ($ _____)

payable under this agreement.

4.   Additional terms and conditions as agreed to by the parties are (if not used

cross out): _____

_____

_____

_____

_____

_____

_____   _____
(Signature of landlord)   (Signature of tenant)

_____   _____
(Signature of landlord)   (Signature of tenant)

GENERAL LEASE

Agreement made _____, 19___, between:
          (month and day)   (yr)

_____   _____
(Name(s) of owner)   (Name(s) of tenant)

hereinafter known as owner, of   hereinafter known as tenant, of

_____   _____
(Address)   (Address)

_____   _____
(City)   (City)

_____   _____
(County)   (County)

_____   _____
(State)   (State)

SECTION ONE - PREMISES- Owner hereby leases to tenant the premises located at:

_____
(Address)

_____
(City)

_____
(County)

_____
(State)

and more particularly described as: _____
                            (insert legal description)

_____ .

The premises shall also include: _____
                      (specify furniture, parking space,

storage space, if any)

_____

Page 1 of 12

GENERAL LEASE - Continued

_____

_____ .

SECTION TWO - TERM- CROSS OUT EITHER PARAGRAPH A OR PARAGRAPH B:

A. Month-to-month: The term of this lease shall begin at _____ ____.m.

o'clock on _____, 19____, and end at _____ ____.m. o'clock
         (month and day)   (yr)

on the last day of the same calendar month. Following such initial period,

the term of this lease shall run from month to month beginning _____,
                                          (month and day)

19____, and shall be automatically renewed for additional periods of one month
  (yr)

thereafter until terminated by either party giving _____ days' written
                                        (number)

notice prior to the end of the rental month. The rental month shall begin

with the due date of the monthly rent.

OR

B. Fixed Term: The term of this lease shall be from _____ ____.m.

o'clock _____, 19____, to _____ ____.m.
       (month and day)   (yr)

o'clock _____, 19____.
       (month and day)   (yr)

No notiice to terminate at the end of such fixed term is necessary unless

otherwise agreed in writing.

If resident retains possession of the premises after expiration of the fixed

lease with the permission of owner, tenant and owner shall continue to be

bound by the terms and conditions of this lease on a month-to-month basis.

The lease may then be terminated by either party giving _____
                                            (number)

days' written notice prior to the end of the rental month.

===

GENERAL LEASE - Continued

C. If the lease term does not begin on the first day of the month, rent shall be prorated to the last day of that month.

SECTION THREE - RENT- CROSS OUT EITHER PARAGRAPH A OR PARAGRAPH B:

A. Month-to-month: If the lease term does not begin on the first day of the month, the first month's prorated rent is _____

Dollars ($_____), due on _____, 19____. The full
   (month and day)   (yr)

monthly rental price for the term of this lease is _____

Dollars ($_____), due on the _____ day of each month
   (number)

beginning _____, 19____. The rental price may not be
   (month and day)   (yr)

changed without _____ days' written notice prior to the end of
   (number)

the rental month.

OR

B. Fixed Term: The total rental price for the term of this lease is

_____ Dollars ($_____). Of this

amount, the first rental payment, in the amount of _____

Dollars ($_____), is due on _____, 19____. The
   (month and day)   (yr)

remainder is payable in monthly installments of _____

Dollars ($_____), due on the _____ day of each month,
   (number)

beginning _____, 19____.
   (month and day)   (yr)

C. Rent payments shall be made to: _____, at
   (Name)

GENERAL LEASE - Continued

```
_____
(Address)
```

```
_____
(City)
```

```
_____
(County)
```

```
_____.
(State)
```

Tenant shall incur and be charged _____ Dollars ($_____) per

day as late fee for payment of rent received after _____

_____.m. o'clock on the _____ day of the month. Such fee,
(number)

which will be considered additional rent, may be collected immediately by owner

or, at owner's option, such fee may be withheld from tenant's security deposit if

written notice of such intended withholding is provided to tenant within

_____ days of the date that the late fee is incurred. The giving of
(number)

such notice of intent shall not relieve owner of any obligation pertaining to the

security deposit set forth in Section Five of this lease. Late fees may be waived

if owner agrees in writing.

A charge of up to _____ Dollars ($_____)

may be imposed for any tenant's check returned to owner because of insufficient

funds, whether the check is for rent, security deposit, or other payment.

Any late fee and returned check fee shall be a reasonable estimate of the

administrative costs incurred by owner.

SECTION FOUR - NOTICE- Unless otherwise specified in this lease, all notices

provided by this lease shall be in writing and shall be delivered to the other

party personally, or sent by first class mail, postage prepaid, or securely and

conspicuously posted, as follows:

Page 4 of 12

GENERAL LEASE - Continued

To tenant: at the premises, or at tenant's last known address.

To owner at:

_____
(Address)

_____
(City)

_____
(County)

_____.
(State)

Notice to one tenant shall be deemed notice to all tenants.

SECTION FIVE - SECURITY DEPOSIT-   (Cross out either Paragraph A or Paragraph B)

A. Tenant has paid owner the sum of _____ Dollars
    ($_____) as a security deposit to secure the performance of this
    rental agreement.

OR

B. By optional and mutual agreement between owner and tenant, tenant agrees to
    pay the security deposit, in the total amount of _____
    Dollars ($_____), according to the following payment schedule:
    _____
    (describe payment schedule)

    _____.

C. Any advance or deposit of money, whether termed last month's rent, damage
    deposit, or security deposit, constitutes a security deposit under this
    section.

D. Tenant may not use the security deposit in place of rent without the written
    permission of owner.

GENERAL LEASE - Continued

E. _____ per cent (%_____) interest per annum from

_____, 19____, shall be paid on the amount of the
(month and day)   (yr)

deposit that tenant is entitled to have returned.

F. It is the duty of tenant to return the premises, including any outside areas, yards or driveways required to be maintained by tenant under this lease, to their condition at the commencement of this lease, except for normal wear and tear.

G. Owner shall return the security deposit to tenant within one month after termination of this lease or surrender and acceptance of the premises, whichever occurs last, unless a longer period of time for return of the deposit is specified here: _____ days.
                                    (number)

If actual cause exists for retaining any portion of the security deposit, owner shall provide tenant with a written statement listing the exact reasons for the retention of any portion of the security deposit. When the statement is delivered, it shall be accompanied by payment of the difference between any sum deposited and the amount retained. Owner is deemed to have complied with this paragraph G by mailing said statement and any payment required to the last known address of tenant. The failure of owner to provide a written statement within the period of time stated above shall work a forfeiture of all owner's rights to withhold any portion of the security deposit.

H. Owner, at owner's option, may use tenant's security deposit during the term of this lease to fulfill tenant's obligations under this lease.

GENERAL LEASE - Continued

SECTION SIX - EVICTION/HOLDING OVER-

A. Owner may evict tenant from the premises or undertake other legal action to regain possession for non-payment of rent or substantial breach of the lease.

B. Tenant shall continue to be liable for rent and be bound by the other provisions of this lease during the time tenant remains in possession of the leased premises even though owner has chosen to seek eviction because of tenant's breach of this lease.

C. If the premises are abandoned or if tenant is evicted, tenant will remain liable for any loss of rent for the remainder of the lease term. Owner will attempt to re-rent the premises to minimize any loss.

D. If tenant does not leave at the end of the lease term and another tenant is waiting to move in, owner, after notifying tenant, may remove tenant's belongings, so long as there is no breach of the peace. Owner will exercise reasonable care in moving and storage of tenant's belongings.

SECTION SEVEN - OCCUPANCY- No more than _____ may reside
                                                    (number)

in the leased premises. Tenant shall not allow guests to stay upon the premises
more than _____ days per month without written consent of
         (number)
the owner.

SECTION EIGHT - USE- Tenant shall use the premises for residential purposes only unless otherwise agreed in writing. Resident shall not engage in any illegal activities on the premises.

SECTION NINE - UTILITIES- Tenant shall be responsible for paying for the following utilities or services connected with the premises (check those applicable):

GENERAL LEASE - Continued

a) _____ water   e) _____ phone (if desired)

b) _____ sewer   f) _____ trash pick-up

c) _____ electricity   g) _____
                                     (other)

d) _____ gas   h) _____
                                     (other)

Within three (3) business days after the beginning of the lease term, tenant shall arrange for such utilities or services and for billing directly to tenant, unless otherwise agreed here: _____
(list exceptions)

_____.

Provision of and payment for utilities and services listed above but not checked shall be the responsibility of owner. The party responsible for any particular utility or service shall not be liable for failure to furnish the utility or service when the cause of such failure is beyond that party's control.

SECTION TEN - PRIVACY- Tenant shall permit owner to enter the premises at reasonable times and upon reasonable notice for the purpose of making necessary or convenient repairs or reasonable inspections, or to show the premises to prospective tenants, purchasers, or lenders. Entry may be made without prior notice only if owner reasonably believes that an emergency exists, such as a fire or broken water pipe, or that the premises have been abandoned.

SECTION ELEVEN - ASSIGNMENT/SUBLEASING/RELEASE- Tenant shall not assign this lease, or sublet any portion of the leased premises, for any part or all of the term of this lease without prior written consent of owner. Owner agrees to release tenant from this lease if tenant finds a replacement tenant, acceptable to owner, who will sign a new lease for the remaining term. Owner shall exercise good faith and reasonableness in accepting a replacement tenant.

GENERAL LEASE - Continued

SECTION TWELVE - NOISE AND NUISANCE- Tenant agrees not to make any excessive noise or to create any nuisance such as will disturb the peace and quiet of neighbors.

SECTION THIRTEEN - RULES AND REGULATIONS- Tenant agrees to abide by all rules and regulations in effect at the time of signing this lease (a copy of which is attached to and hereby made part of this lease) and to such ammended rules or regulations which tenant agrees to in writing.

SECTION FOURTEEN - CHECK-IN/CHECK-OUT SHEET- A check-in/check-out sheet

_____ attached to this lease. Both parties should complete and
(is/is not)

sign this sheet within _____ days of occupancy.
                           (number)

SECTION FIFTEEN - FURNISHINGS- If the premises are furnished, a separate inventory of the furnishings, including their condition, may be attached to this lease. Both parties should complete and sign this form within _____
                                                                    (number)
days of occupancy.

SECTION SIXTEEN - REPAIRS AND MAINTENANCE- If repairs are required in order for the premises to be in compliance with the _____ Housing
                                                    (name of city)
Code, owner shall be responsible for making such repairs. _____
                                                              (Owner/Tenant)
shall be responsible for payment of any costs of such repairs unless the repairs were necessitated by the negligence or willful acts of the other party to this lease.

Tenant shall not make any repairs without prior written consent of owner.

Tenant shall pay reasonable charges, other than for normal wear and tear, for the repair of damage to the premises or common areas caused by the negligence or willful acts of tenant, members of tenant's household, or guests. Excessive

Page 9 of 12

GENERAL LEASE - Continued

damage to the premises by tenant, members of tenant's household, or guests, shall be grounds for owner to evict tenant.

SECTION SEVENTEEN - CONSTRUCTIVE EVICTION- When conditions beyond the control of tenant cause the premises to become legally unihabitable, and when owner is responsible for remedying those conditions but does not do so within a reasonable time after notification by tenant, tenant may vacate the premises, terminate this lease, and owe no future rent.

SECTION EIGHTEEN - OUTSIDE MAINTENANCE- Tenant shall be responsible for the routine care and maintenance of the yard and outside areas as follows (check those applicable):

a) _____ mowing lawn

b) _____ watering lawn, trees and shrubs

c) _____ removing weeds

d) _____ raking leaves

e) removing snow and ice from:

_____ sidewalks and walkways

_____ driveways

_____ parking area

_____
(other)

The routine care and maintenance of items listed above but not checked shall be the reponsibility of owner.

Tenant's obligation to perform any task set forth in this paragraph above is subject to owner supplying tenant with equipment appropriate to the task as follows (check those applicable):

a) _____ lawn mower

b) _____ hoses and sprinklers

c) _____ rake

d) _____ snow shovel

e) _____
(other)

SECTION NINETEEN - ALTERATIONS TO PREMISES- Tenant agrees that before making alterations to the premises including, for example, painting, adding or changing

Page 10 of 12

door locks, or altering landscaping, advance written consent of owner will be obtained.

SECTION TWENTY - PETS- No pets shall be allowed without the prior written consent of owner.

SECTION TWENTY-ONE - PARKING- Tenant's parking rights are defined as follows:

_____

_____

_____ .

SECTION TWENTY-TWO - INSURANCE- Owner's insurance does not cover tenant's personal possessions in the event of loss or damage due to fire, windstorm, flood, theft, vandalism, or other similar cause. If tenant desires to insure personal possessions or to insure against tenant's personal liability, tenant's insurance should be obtained.

SECTION TWENTY-THREE - ATTORNEYS' FEES- In the event of any legal action concerning this lease which results in a judgement, the losing party shall pay to the prevailing party reasonable attorneys' fees and court costs to be fixed by the court.

SECTION TWENTY-FOUR - SUBORDINATION- This lease shall be subordinate to all existing and future mortgages and deeds of trust upon the property.

SECTION TWENTY-FIVE - WAIVER- Any waiver, by either party of any breach of any provision of this lease shall not be considered to be a continuing waiver of a subsequent breach of the same or a different provision of this lease.

GENERAL LEASE - Continued

SECTION TWENTY-SIX - SEVERABILITY- The unenforceability of any provision or provisions of this lease shall not affect the enforceability of any other provision or provisions.

SECTION TWENTY-SEVEN - JOINT AND SEVERAL LIABILITY- If this lease is signed on behalf of tenant by more than one person, then the liability of the persons so signing shall be joint and several.

SECTION TWENTY-EIGHT - SIGNATURES/AMMENDMENT OF LEASE- This lease contains the entire agreement of the parties and may not be altered or ammended except by mutual written agreement signed by both parties.

Signed this _____ day of _____, 19____.
      (number)   (month)   (yr)

_____
(Signature of Owner)

_____
(Signature of Owner)

_____
(Signature of Owner)

_____
(Signature of Tenant)

_____
(Signature of Tenant)

_____
(Signature of Tenant)

_____
(Signature of Tenant)

If required by state law, signatures of two witnesses for owner and two witnesses for tenant should sign this agreement.

_____
(Witness for owner)

_____
(Witness for owner)

_____
(Witness for tenant)

_____
(Witness for tenant)

LEASE/RENTAL AGREEMENT: MONTH-TO-MONTH TENANCY

Agreement made _____ , 19____ , between:
               (month and day)   (yr)

_____ and _____
(Name(s) of landlord)   (Name(s) of tenant)

herein known as landlord, of   herein known as tenant, of

_____   _____
(Address)   (Address)

_____   _____
(City)   (City)

_____   _____
(County)   (County)

_____   _____
(State)   (State)

RECITALS -

Landlord rents to tenant, and tenant hires from landlord for use as a residence a

_____   _____
(furnished/unfurnished)   (apartment/flat/as the case may be)

located at   _____
                      (Address)

                      _____
                      (City)

                      _____
                      (County)

                      _____.
                      (State)

The above described property is leased to tenant for tenancy from month to month

commencing on _____ , 19____ , on the following terms and conditions:
         (month and day)   (yr)

MONTH-TO-MONTH LEASE - Continued

SECTION ONE - RENTAL - Tenant agrees to pay as rental for the demised premises

_____ Dollars ($_____) per month, payable, without demand, in

advance on the _____ day of each month. The first and last months'
          (number)

rental is paid on the execution of this agreement, receipt of which is

acknowledged by landlord.

SECTION TWO - SECURITY DEPOSIT - On execution of this agreement, tenant deposits

with landlord the additional sum of _____ Dollars ($_____),

receipt of which is acknowledged by landlord, as security for the full and

faithful performance by tenant of the terms hereof, to be returned to the tenant

without interest, on the full and faithful performance of the tenant of the

provisions hereof stated.

SECTION THREE - FURNISHINGS - Cross out either Paragraph A or Paragraph B:

A. The _____ is leased as a furnished unit
       (apartment/flat/or as case may be)

containing the items of household furniture, kitchen utensils, and other household

items listed in Schedule "A" attached hereto and made a part hereof. No

furnishings or other household items are furnished or leased with the unit other

than those listed in such schedule. Tenant agrees to return all items listed in

the schedule to landlord on the expiration of the tenancy in as good condition as

when received, reasonable wear and tear excepted. Tenant by the execution of this

agreement accepts all items listed in the schedule as being good, serviceable

condition. Tenant will be responsible for all breakage or other damage to items

listed. (Chipped, cracked, or burned dishes will be counted as breakage).

OR

Page 2 of 6

MONTH-TO-MONTH LEASE - Continued

B. The _____ is leased as an unfurnished unit.
    (apartment/flat/as case may be)

SECTION FOUR - UTILITIES - Tenant shall be responsible for paying for the following utilities or services connected with the premises (check those applicable):

_____ water   _____ phone

_____ sewer   _____ trash removal

_____ electricity   _____ other _____

_____ gas   _____ other _____

SECTION FIVE - OCCUPANCY - Tenant agrees that the demised premises shall be occupied by no more than _____ persons, consisting of _____
                                  (number)   (number)
adults and _____ children without the written permission of landlord.
            (number)

Tenant shall not keep or permit to be kept on the premises any animal, bird, or other pet without landlord's written consent, except _____
                                                                   (list exceptions)

_____

_____.

SECTION SIX - RIGHT OF ENTRY - Landlord reserves the right to enter the demised premises at all reasonable hours for the purpose of inspection, and whenever necessary to make repairs and alterations to the demised premises. Tenant hereby grants permission to landlord to show the demised premises to new rental applicants at reasonable hours of the day, within _____ days of the
                                                              (number)
expiration of the tenancy.

Page 3 of 6

MONTH-TO-MONTH LEASE - Continued

SECTION SEVEN - ASSIGNMENT AND SUBLETTING - Tenant shall not sublet the demised premises, or any part thereof, or assign this agreement without landlord's written consent.

SECTION EIGHT - DEFAULT - Any failure by tenant to pay rent or other charges promptly when due or to comply with any other term or condition hereof shall, at the option of landlord, forthwith terminate this tenancy and forfeit all rights of tenant under this agreement.

SECTION NINE - MAINTENANCE AND REDELIVERY - Tenant shall keep and maintain the demised premises in a clean and sanitary condition at all times, and on the expiration or sooner termination of the tenancy shall surrender the premises to landlord in as good condition as when received, ordinary wear and tear and damage by the elements excepted.

SECTION TEN - DUTY TO REPAIR - Landlord shall put the demised premises into condition fit for occupation by the commencement of the tenancy, and shall repair all subsequent dilapidations thereof which may render them untenantable

as defined in _____ of the _____,
            (appropriate code section)   (appropriate state code)

except that tenant shall repair all deteriorations or injuries to the demised premises occasioned by tenant's want of ordinary care or greater degree of culpability. No duty on the part of landlord shall arise with respect to repairs for tenantability under this section, however, if tenant is in substantial violation of any one or more of the following affirmative obligations:

(a) To keep the demised premises clean and sanitary as the condition of same permits.

(b) To remove from the dwelling unit all rubbish, garbage, and other waste, in a clean and sanitary manner.

(c) To properly use and operate all electrical, gas, and plumbing fixtures and to keep them as clean and sanitary as their condition permits.

(d) To not allow any person on the premises, with tenant's permission, to willfully or wantonly destroy, deface, damage, impair, or remove any part of the structure or dwelling unit or the facilities, equipment, furnishings, or appurtenances thereto, nor will tenant do any such thing.

(e) To occupy the premises as an abode, utilizing the portions thereof for living, sleeping, cooking, or dining purposes only which were respectively designed or intended to be used for such occupancies.

SECTION ELEVEN - HOLD OVER - The parties agree that any holding over by tenant under this agreement, without landlord's written consent, shall be a tenancy at will which may be terminated by landlord on _____ days' notice in
                                                            (number)
writing thereof.

SECTION TWELVE - TERMINATION - This agreement and the tenancy hereby granted may be terminated at any time by either party giving to the other party not less than

_____ days' prior written notice. In the event there are two or more
(number)

tenants named herein, service of such notice by landlord on any one of the tenants named herein shall be construed, and tenants hereby agree that such service shall be construed, as effective service of notice of termination of tenancy on all tenants residing on the premises.

MONTH-TO-MONTH LEASE - Continued

SECTION THIRTEEN - ATTORNEYS' FEES - If suit is brought by landlord for an unlawful detainer of the demised premises, for the recovery of any rent due under the provisions of this agreement, or for any obligation of tenant arising under this agreement or by law, then tenant hereby agrees to pay landlord all the costs in connection therewith, including, but not limited to, reasonable attorneys' fees, whether or not the action or actions proceed to judgment.

In witness whereof, the parties have executed this agreement in the City of
_____ , State of _____ ,
the day and year first above written.

_____
(Signature of landlord)

(Signature of tenant)

_____
(Signature of landlord)

(Signature of tenant)

If required by state law, two witnesses for landlord and two witness for tenant should sign this agreement.

_____
(Witness for landlord)

(Witness for tenant)

_____
(Witness for landlord)

(Witness for tenant)

LEASE OF FURNISHED APARTMENT

Agreement made _____, 19____, between:
(month and day)   (yr)

_____   and   _____
(Name(s) of tenant)   (Name(s) of landlord)

herein referred to as tenant, of   herein referred to as landlord, of

_____   _____
(Address)   (Address)

_____   _____
(City)   (City)

_____   _____
(County)   (County)

_____   _____
(State)   (State)

SECTION ONE - DESCRIPTION OF APARTMENT- Landlord leases to tenant, and tenant

leases from landlord, apartment No._____, on the _____ floor of the
(number)

building called _____, located at
(name of building)

_____
(Address)

_____
(City)

_____
(County)

_____,
(State)

and all the goods and chattels detailed in the inventory designated Schedule "A"

annexed hereto and specifically made a part hereof. The apartment consists of

_____ rooms, including _____ bedrooms, and _____
(number)   (number)   (number)

baths, and _____
(describe other rooms)

_____.

LEASE OF FURNISHED APARTMENT - Continued

SECTION TWO - OCCUPANCY- The apartment is leased for occupancy as a private

dwelling to tenant and tenant's family, consisting of _____,
                                                        (number of persons)

and is not to be used for may other purpose or occupied by any other person, other

than transient relatives and friends who are guests of tenant, without first

obtaining landlord's written consent to such use.

SECTION THREE - TERM- The apartment is leased for a term of _____
                                                               (number)

_____ beginning _____, 19____, and
(months/years)   (month and day)   (yr)

ending _____, 19____, at _____ o'clock ____.m.
       (month and day)   (yr)

SECTION FOUR - RENT- The total rent for the apartment is _____

Dollars ($_____), payable on the _____ day of each month of the
                                     (number)

term, in equal installments of _____ Dollars ($_____), first

and last installments to be paid on the execution of this lease, second

installment to be paid on _____, 19___.
                          (month and day)   (yr)

SECTION FIVE - CLEANING FEE- Tenant agrees to pay landlord a cleaning fee of

_____ Dollars ($_____), payable on the execution of this

lease, which fee is not refundable.

SECTION SIX - FURNISHINGS - The apartment is leased as a furnished apartment

containing the items of household furniture, kitchen utensils, and other household

items lised in Schedule "A" attached hereto and made a part hereof. No

furnishings or other household items are furnished or leased with the apartment

LEASE OF FURNISHED APARTMENT - Continued

other than those listed in such schedule. Tenant agrees to return all items listed in the schedule to landlord at the end of the term of this lease in as good condition as when received, reasonable wear and tear excepted. Tenant by the execution of this lease accepts all items listed in the schedule as being in good, serviceable condition. Tenant will be responsible for all breakage or other damage to items listed. Chipped, cracked, or burned dishes will be counted as breakage.

SECTION SEVEN - SHOWING APARTMENT FOR RENTAL- Tenant hereby grants permission to landlord to show the apartment to new rental applicants at reasonable hours of the day, within _____ days of the expiration of the term of this lease.
(number)

SECTION EIGHT - ENTRY FOR INSPECTION, REPAIRS, AND ALTERATIONS - Landlord shall have the right to enter the leased premises for inspection thereof at all reasonable hours and whenever necessary to make repairs and alterations of the apartment or the building, or to clean the apartment.

SECTION NINE - UTILITES- Tenant shall be responsible for paying the following utilities or services connected with the premises (check those applicable):

_____ water

_____ sewer

_____ electricity

_____ gas

_____ phone

_____ trash pick up

_____ Other: _____

_____ Other: _____

SECTION TEN - LAUNDRY- Expense of laundering sheets, blankets, and other bedding, curtains, drapes, and other items furnished, shall be borne by tenant.

LEASE OF FURNISHED APARTMENT - Continued

SECTION ELEVEN - ANIMALS - Tenant shall keep no domestic or other animals in or about the apartment or on the apartment-house premises without the written consent of landlord.

SECTION TWELVE - WASTE, NUISANCE, OR UNLAWFUL USE- Tenant agrees that tenant will not commit waste on the premises, or maintain or permit to be maintained a nuisance thereon, or use or permit the premises to be used in an unlawful manner.

SECTION THIRTEEN - WAIVERS- Waiver by landlord of any breach or any covenant or duty of tenant under this lease is not a waiver of a breach of any other covenant or duty of tenant, or of any subsequent breach of the same covenant or duty.

SECTION FOURTEEN - ASSIGNMENT OF SUBLEASE- Tenant shall not assign this lease, or sublet the apartment hereby leased or any part of tenant's interest thereof, without prior written consent of landlord. Landlord reserves the right to assign landlord's interest in this lease, and any sums received hereunder, on sale or release of the apartment building.

SECTION FIFTEEN - TENANT'S HOLDING OVER- The parties agree that any holding over by tenant under this lease, without landlord's written consent, shall be a tenancy at will which may be terminated by landlord on _____ days'
(number)
notice in writing thereof.

SECTION SIXTEEN - STORAGE- Cross out either Paragraph A or Paragraph B:

   A. No right of storage is given by this lease.

OR

===

LEASE OF FURNISHED APARTMENT - Continued

B. Tenant is hereby given permission to store articles in _____
(describe

_____

storage location)

during the term of this lease. Landlord shall not be liable for loss of or

damage to the goods so stored. Tenant shall not remove items stored until

all amounts due under this lease have been paid.

SECTION SEVENTEEN - PARKING SPACE- Tenant is hereby granted a license to use

parking space No. _____ in the building or in the building parking lot for

the purpose of parking _____ motor vehicle(s) during the term of
(number of vehicles)

this lease.

SECTION EIGHTEEN - REPAIRS, REDECORATION, OR ALTERATIONS- Landlord shall be

responsible for repairs to the interior and exterior of the building, provided,

however, that repairs required through damage caused by tenant shall be charged to

tenant as additional rent. It is agreed that tenant will not make or permit to be

made any alterations, additions, improvements, or changes in the premises without

in each case first obtaining the written consent of landlord. A consent to a

particular alteration, addition, improvement, or change shall not be deemed a

consent to or a waiver of restriction against alterations, additions,

improvements, or changes for the future.

SECTION NINETEEN - OPTION TO RENEW- Tenant is hereby granted the option of

renewing this lease for an additional term of _____ _____
(number)   (months/years)

upon the same terms and conditions as contained herein and at the _____
(monthly/annual)

rent of _____ Dollars ($_____). If tenant elects to exercise

this option tenant must give at least _____ days' written notice to
(number)

landlord prior to the expiration date of this lease.

LEASE OF FURNISHED APARTMENT - Continued

SECTION TWENTY - REDELIVERY OF PREMISES- At the end of the term of this lease, tenant shall quit and deliver up the premises to landlord in as good condition as as they are now, ordinary wear, decay, and damage by the elements excepted.

SECTION TWENTY-ONE - DESTRUCTION OF PREMISES AND EMINENT DOMAIN- If the premises are destroyed substantially by fire or taken by eminent domain, either party may terminate this lease without liability for the remainder of the term. A condemnation award shall belong exclusively to landlord.

SECTION TWENTY-TWO - DEFAULT- If tenant defaults in the payment of rent or any part thereof at the times hereinbefore specified, or if tenant defaults in the performance of or compliance with any other term or condition hereof of the regulations attached hereto and made a part hereof, which regulations shall be subject to occasional amendment or addition by landlord, the lease, at the option of landlord, shall terminate and be forfeited, and landlord may re-enter the premises and retake possession and recover damages, including costs and attorneys' fees. Tenant shall be given _____ days' written notice of any
(number)
default or breach, and termination and forfeiture of the lease shall not result if, within _____ days after receipt of such notice, tenant has
(number)
corrected the default or breach or has taken action reasonably likely to effect such correction within a reasonable time.

SECTION TWENTY-THREE - LAW GOVERNING DISPUTES- The parties agree that the law of the State of _____ will govern all disputes under this lease, and determine all rights hereunder.

Page 6 of 7

SECTION TWENTY-FOUR - BINDING EFFECT- The covenants and conditions herein contained shall apply to and bind the heirs, legal representatives, and assigns of the parties hereto, and all covenants are to be construed as conditions of this lease.

In witness whereof, the parties have executed this lease in the City of

_____ , State of _____ ,

the day and the year first above written.

_____   _____
(Signature of landlord)   (Signature of tenant)

_____   _____
(Signature of landlord)   (Signature of tenant)

If required by state law, two witnesses for landlord and two witnesses for tenant should sign this agreement:

_____   _____
(Witness for landlord)   (Witness for tenant)

_____   _____
(Witness for landlord)   (Witness for tenant)

LEASE OF FURNISHED HOUSE

Agreement made _____, 19____, between:
(month and day)   (yr)

_____   and   _____
(Name(s) of landlord)   (Name(s) of tenant)

herein referred to as landlord, of   herein referred to as tenant, of

_____   _____
(Address)   (Address)

_____   _____
(City)   (City)

_____   _____
(County)   (County)

_____   _____
(State)   (State)

Landlord leases to tenant all the goods and chattels detailed in the

inventory designated Schedule "A" annexed hereto and specifically made a part

hereof, and also that certain dwelling house situated at

_____
(Address)

_____
(City)

_____
(County)

_____
(State)

and more particularly described as follows: _____
(legal description)

_____

together with all appurtenances, for a term of _____ years, to commence on
(number)

_____, 19____, at _____ o'clock _____. m.
(month and day)   (yr)

LEASE OF FURNISHED HOUSE - Continued

SECTION ONE - RENT- Tenant agrees to pay, without demand, to landlord as rent for the demised premises and the goods and chattels detailed in Schedule "A", or any amendment thereof, the sum of _____ Dollars ($_____) per month in advance on the _____ day of each calendar month beginning
                      (number)

_____, 19____, at
(month and day)   (yr)

_____
(Address)

_____
(City)

_____
(County)

_____
(State)

or such other place as landlord may designate.

SECTION TWO - SECURITY DEPOSIT- On execution of this lease, tenant deposits with landlord _____ Dollars ($_____), receipt of which is acknowledged by landlord, as security for the faithful performance by tenant of the terms hereof, to be returned to tenant, without interest, on the full and faithful performance by tenant of the provisions hereof.

SECTION THREE- CLEANING FEE- On the execution of this lease, tenant deposits with landlord the additional sum of _____ Dollars ($_____), receipt of which is acknowledged by landlord, as a cleaning fee to be applied as landlord deems reasonably necessary at the expiration or sooner termination of this lease to provide for the cleaning of the demised dwelling house and the

_____
(carpeting, drapes, furniture, and appliances listed in Schedule "A"

_____.
or as the case may be)

Page 2 of 9

LEASE OF FURNISHED HOUSE - Continued

After landlord's determination of the amount reasonably necessary to accomplish this end, the remainder of the cleaning fee, if any, shall be returned to tenant without interest. Tenant stipulates that tenant has examined the goods and chattels detailed in Schedule "A" and that they are, at the date of this lease, in good order, repair, and a safe and clean condition.

SECTION FOUR - USE OF GOODS AND CHATTELS- Tenant covenants that tenant will carefully and economically use the goods and chattels detailed in Schedule "A", as such schedule currently exists and as such may be amended from time to time by written agreement between landlord and tenant, and tenant further covenants that tenant will not transfer the use or possession of such goods and chattels, or any part of the same, to any person or persons whomsoever, without the written consent of landlord; that tenant will forthwith repair all injury and pay all damages that may happen or accrue to such goods and chattels, or any part thereof, during the term of this lease; that tenant will not remove or allow any of such goods and chattels to be removed from the demised premises to any other place (removal from danger by fire excepted), without the written consent of landlord; that tenant will not encumber or allow any liens to be attached to such goods and chattels; and that tenant will at the expiration or sooner termination of this lease surrender the goods and chattels detailed in Schedule "A" or any amended schedule to landlord or landlord's agent in as good state and condition as when the same are received, ordinary wear alone excepted, and subject to the provisions of SECTION THREE above.

SECTION FIVE - USE OF PREMISES- The demised premises shall be used and occupied by tenant exclusively as a private single-family residence, and neither the premises nor any part thereof shall be used by tenant at any time during the term

LEASE OF FURNISHED HOUSE - Continued

of this lease for the purpose of carrying on any business, profession, or trade of any kind, or for any purpose other than as a private single-family residence. Tenant shall comply with all the sanitary laws, ordinances, rules, and orders of appropriate governmental authorities affecting the cleanliness, occupancy, and preservation of the demised premises, and the sidewalks connected thereto, during the term of this lease.

SECTION SIX - NUMBER OF OCCUPANTS- Lesee agrees that the demised premises shall be occupied by no more than _____ persons, consisting of _____
                                                 (number)   (number)
adults and _____ children under the age of _____ years, without
            (number)   (number)
the written consent of landlord.

SECTION SEVEN - CONDITION OF PREMISES- Tenant stipulates that tenant has examined the demised premises, including the grounds and all buildings and improvements, and that they are, at the date of this lease, in good order, repair, and a safe, clean and tenantable condition.

SECTION EIGHT - ASSIGNMENT AND SUBLETTING- Without the prior written consent of landlord, tenant shall not assign this lease, or sublet or grant any concession or license to use the premises or any part thereof. A consent by landlord to one assignment, subletting, concession, or license shall not be deemed to be a consent to any subsequent assignment, subletting, concession, or license. An assignment, subletting, concession, or license without the prior written consent of landlord, or an assignment or subletting by operation of law, shall be void and shall, at landlord's option, terminate this lease.

LEASE OF FURNISHED HOUSE - Continued

SECTION NINE - ALTERATIONS AND IMPROVEMENTS- Tenant shall make no alterations to the buildings on the demised premises or construct any building or make other improvements on the demised premises without the prior written consent of landlord. All alterations, changes, and improvements built, constructed, or placed on the demised premises by tenant, with the exception of fixtures removable without damage to the premises and movable personal property, shall, unless otherwise provided by written agreement between landlord and tenant, be the property of landlord and remain on the demised premises at the expiration or sooner termination of this lease.

SECTION TEN - DAMAGE TO PREMISES- If the leased premises, or any part thereof, shall be partially damaged by fire or other casualty not due to tenant's negligence or willful act or that of tenant's employee, family, or guests, the premises shall be promptly repaired by landlord and there shall be an abatement of rent corresponding with the time during which, the extent to which, the leased premises may have been untenantable; but, if the leased premises should be damaged other than by tenant's negligence or willful act or that of tenant's employee, family, or guests to the extent that landlord shall decide not to rebuild or repair, the term of this lease shall end and the rent shall be prorated up to the time of the damage.

SECTION ELEVEN - DANGEROUS MATERIALS- Tenant shall not keep or have on the leased premises any article or thing of a dangerous, inflammable, or explosive character that might unreasonably increase the danger of fire on the leased premises, or that might be considered hazardous or extra hazardous by any responsible insurance company.

LEASE OF FURNISHED HOUSE - Continued

SECTION TWELVE - UTILITIES- Tenant shall be responsible for paying for the following utilities and services connected with the premises (check those applicable):

_____ water   _____ phone

_____ sewer   _____ trash pick up

_____ electricity   _____ Other: _____

_____ gas   _____ Other: _____

SECTION THIRTEEN - MAINTENANCE AND REPAIR- Tenant will, at tenant's sole expense, keep and maintain the leased premises and appurtenances in good and sanitary condition and repair during the term of this lease and any renewal thereof, except as specified otherwise herein. In particular, tenant shall keep the fixtures in the house or on or about the leased premises in good order and repair; keep the furnace clean; keep the electric bells in order; keep the walks free from dirt and debris; and, at tenant's sole expense, shall make all required repairs to the plumbing, range, heating apparatus, and electric and gas fixtures whenever damage thereto shall have resulted from tenant's misuse, waste, or neglect or that of tenant's employee, family, or guests. Major maintenance and repair of the leased premises involving anticipated or actual costs in excess of _____ Dollars ($_____) per incident not due to tenant's misuse, waste, or neglect or that of tenant's employee, family, or guests, shall be the responsibility of landlord or landlord's assigns. Tenant agrees that no signs shall be placed or painting done on or about the leased premises by tenant or at tenant's direction without the prior written consent of landlord.

SECTION FOURTEEN - ANIMALS- Tenant shall keep no domestic or other animals on or about the leased premises without the written consent of landlord.

LEASE OF FURNISHED HOUSE - Continued

SECTION FIFTEEN - RIGHT OF INSPECTION- Landlord shall have the right at all reasonable times during the term of this lease and any renewal thereof to enter the demised premises for the purpose of inspecting the demised premises and all buildings and improvements thereon, and all goods and chattels as detailed in Schedule "A" or any amendment thereof.

SECTION SIXTEEN - DISPLAY OF SIGNS- During the last _____ days of this
                                                          (number)
lease, landlord or landlord's agent shall have the privilege of displaying the usual "For Sale" or "For Rent" or "Vacancy" signs on the demised premises and of showing the property to prospective purchasers or tenants.

SECTION SEVENTEEN - SUBORDINATION OF LEASE- This lease and tenant's leasehold interest hereunder are and shall be subject, subordinate, and inferior to any liens or encumbrances now or hereafter placed on the demised premises by landlord, all advances made under any such liens or encumbrances, the interest payable on any such liens or encumbrances, and any and all renewals or extensions of such liens or encumbrances.

SECTION EIGHTEEN - HOLDOVER BY TENANT- Should tenant remain in possession of the demised premises with the consent of landlord after the natural expiration of this lease, a new tenancy from month to month shall be created between landlord and tenant which shall be subject to all the terms and conditions hereof but which shall be terminable by _____ days' written notice served by either
                              (number)
landlord or tenant on the other party.

LEASE OF FURNISHED HOUSE - Continued

SECTION NINETEEN - SURRENDER OF PREMISES- At the expiration of the lease term, tenant shall quit and surrender the premises hereby demised in as good state and condition as they were at the commencement of this lease, reasonable use and wear thereof and damages by the elements excepted.

SECTION TWENTY - DEFAULT- If any default is made in the payment of rent, or any part thereof, at the times hereinbefore specified, or if any default is made in the performance of or compliance with any other term or condition hereof, this lease, at the option of landlord, shall terminate and be forfeited, and landlord may re-enter the premises and remove all persons therefrom. Tenant shall be given

_____ days' written notice of any default or breach, and termination
(number)

and forfeiture of the lease shall not result if, within _____ days of
                                                        (number)

receipt of such notice, tenant has corrected the default or breach or has taken action reasonably likely to effect such correction within a reasonable time.

SECTION TWENTY-ONE - ABANDONMENT- If any time during the term of this lease tenant abandons the demised premises or any part thereof, landlord may, at landlord's option, enter the demised premises by any means without being liable for any prosecution therefor, and without becoming liable to tenant for damages or for any payment of any kind whatever, and may, at landlord's discretion, as agent for tenant, re-rent the demised premises, or any part thereof, for the whole or any part of the then unexpired term, and may receive and collect all rent payable by virtue of such re-renting and, at landlord's option hold tenant liable for any difference between the rent that would have been payable under this lease during the balance of the unexpired term, if this lease had continued in force, and the net rent for such period realized by landlord by means of such re-renting.

LEASE OF FURNISHED HOUSE - Continued

If landlord's right of re-entry is exercised following abandonment of the premises by tenant, then landlord may consider any personal property belonging to tenant and left on the premises to also have been abandoned, in which case landlord may dispose of all such personal property in any manner landlord shall deem proper and is hereby relieved of all liability for doing so.

SECTION TWENTY-TWO - BINDING EFFECT- The covenants and conditions herein contained shall apply to and bind the heirs, legal representatives, and assigns of the parties hereto, and all covenants are to be construed as conditions of this lease.

In witness whereof, the parties have executed this lease in the City of

_____ , State of _____ ,

the day and the year first above written.

_____   _____
(Signature of landlord)   (Signature of tenant)

_____   _____
(Signature of landlord)   (Signature of tenant)

If required by state law, two witnesses for landlord and two witnesses for tenant should sign this agreement:

_____   _____
(Witness for landlord)   (Witness for tenant)

_____   _____
(Witness for landlord)   (Witness for tenant)

LEASE/RENTAL AGREEMENT AND DEPOSIT RECEIPT

Agreement made _____, 19___, between:
          (month and day)   (yr)

_____ and	_____
(Name(s) of owner)	(Name(s) of tenant)
herein referred to as owner, of	herein referred to as tenant, of
_____	_____
(Address)	(Address)
_____	_____
(City)	(City)
_____	_____
(County)	(County)
_____	_____
(State)	(State)

RECEIVED FROM _____ the sum of _____

Dollars ($_____) evidenced by _____,
                            (cash, personal check, cashier's check, etc.)

as a deposit which upon acceptance of this rental agreement, the owner of the

premises shall apply said deposit as follows:

	RECEIVED	PAYABLE PRIOR TO OCCUPANCY
Rent for the period		
from _____, 19___		
(month and day) (yr)		
to _____, 19___		
(month and day) (yr)	$_____	$_____
_____ of		
(full/ half)		
last month's rent	$_____	$_____
Security deposit	$_____	$_____
Other	$_____	$_____
TOTAL	$_____	$_____

LEASE/RENTAL AND DEPOSIT RECEIPT - Continued

In the event that this agrement is not accepted by the owner within

_____ days, the total deposit received shall be refunded.
(number)

Tenant hereby offers to rent from the owner the premises situated at

_____
(Address)

_____
(City)

_____
(County)

_____.
(State)

described as: _____
 (legal description of premises)

_____,

consisting of: _____
 (describe exact real and personal property)

_____,

upon the following terms and conditions:

SECTION ONE - TERM- The term hereof shall commence on _____, 19____,
 (month and day)   (yr)

and continue: (choose either Paragraph A or Paragraph B)

A. _____ until _____, 19____
 (month and day)   (yr)

OR

B. _____ on a month-to-month basis thereafter, until either party shall

terminate the same by giving the other party _____ days'
 (number)

written notice delivered by certified mail, provided that tenant

agrees not to terminate prior to the expiration of _____
 (number)

months.

LEASE/RENTAL AND DEPOSIT RECEIPT - Continued

SECTION TWO - RENT- Rent shall be _____ Dollars ($_____) per month, payable in advance, upon the _____ day of each calendar month

                          (number)

to owner at the following address:

_____
(Address)

_____
(City)

_____
(County)

_____
(State)

or at such other places as may be designated by owner from time to time. In event rent is not paid within _____ days after due date, tenant agrees to pay

                          (number)

a late charge of _____ Dollars ($_____) plus interest at _____ per cent (_____%) per annum on the delinquent amount.

SECTION THREE - MULTIPLE OCCUPANCY- It is expressly understood that this agreement is between the owner and each signatory individually and severally. In the event of default by any one signatory each and every remaining signatory shall be responsible for timely payment of rent and all other provisions of this agreement.

SECTION FOUR - UTILITIES- Tenant shall be responsible for payment of all utilities and services, except _____

                          (specific utilities and services)

_____

which shall be paid by owner.

LEASE/RENTAL AND DEPOSIT RECEIPT - Continued

SECTION FIVE - USE- The premises shall be used as a residence by the undersigned tenant with no more than _____ adults and _____ children and
          (number)   (number)

for no other purpose, without the prior written consent of the owner. Occupancy by guests staying over _____ days will be considered to be in
                          (number)

violation of this provision .

SECTION SIX - PETS- No pets shall be brought on the premises without the prior written consent of the owner.

SECTION SEVEN - HOUSE RULES- In the event that the premises are a portion of a building containing more than one unit, tenant agrees to abide by any and all house rules, whether promulgated before or after the execution hereof, including, but not limited to, rules with respect to noise, odors, disposal of refuse, pets, parking, and use of common areas. Tenant shall not have a waterbed on the premises without prior written consent of the owner.

SECTION EIGHT - ORDINANCES AND STATUTES- Tenant shall comply with all statutes, ordinances and requirements of all municipal, state and federal authorities now in force, or which may hereafter be in force, pertaining to the use of the premises.

SECTION NINE - ASSIGNMENT AND SUBLETTING- Tenant shall not assign this agreement or sublet any portion of the premises without prior written consent of the owner, which may not unreasonably be withheld.

SECTION TEN - MAINTENANCE, REPAIRS OR ALTERATIONS- Tenant acknowledges that the premises are in good order and repair, unless otherwise indicated herein. Owner

may at any time give tenant a written inventory of furniture and furnishings on the premises and tenant shall be deemed to have possession of all said furniture and furnishings in good condition and repair, unless tenant objects thereto in writing within _____ days after receipt of such inventory. Tenant
(number)

shall, at tenant's own expense, and at all times maintain the premises in a clean and sanitary manner including all equipment, appliances, furniture and furnishings therein and shall surrender the same, at termination hereof, in as good condition as received, normal wear and tear excepted. Tenant shall be responsible for damages caused by tenant's negligence and that of tenant's family, invitees and guests. Tenant shall not paint, paper or otherwise redecorate or make alterations to the premises without the prior written consent of the owner. Tenant shall irrigate and maintain any surrounding grounds, including lawns and shrubbery, and keep the same clear of rubbish or weeds if such grounds are part of the premises and are exclusively for the use of the tenant.

SECTION ELEVEN - ENTRY AND INSPECTION- Tenant shall permit owner to enter the premises at reasonable times and upon reasonable notice for the purpose of making necessary or convenient repairs, or to show the premises to prospective tenants, purchasers, or mortgagees.

SECTION TWELVE - INDEMNIFICATION- Owner shall not be liable for any damage or injury to tenant, or any other person, or to any property, occurring on the premises, or any part thereof, or in common areas thereof, unless such damage is the proximate result of the negligence or unlawful act of owner or owner's employees. Tenant agrees to hold owner harmless from any claims for damages no matter how caused, except for injury or damamges for which owner is legally responsible.

Page 5 of 9

LEASE/RENTAL AND DEPOSIT RECEIPT - Continued

SECTION THIRTEEN - POSSESSION- If owner is not able to deliver possession of the premises at the commencement hereof, owner shall not be liable for any damage caused therby, nor shall this agreement be void or voidable, but tenant shall not be liable for any rent until possession is delivered. Tenant may terminate this agreement if possession is not delivered within _____ days of the

(number)

commencement of the term hereof.

SECTION FOURTEEN - DEFAULT- If tenant shall fail to pay rent when due, or perform any term hereof, after not less than _____ days' written notice

(number)

of such default given in the manner required by law, the owner, at owner's option, may terminate all rights of tenant hereunder, unless tenant, within said time, shall cure such default. If tenant abandons or vacates the property, while in default of the payment of rent, owner may consider any property left on the premises to be abandoned and may dispose of the same in any manner allowed by law. In the event the owner reasonably believes that such abandoned property has no value, it may be discarded. All property on the premises is hereby subject to a lien in favor of the owner for the payment of all sums due hereunder, to the maximum extent allowed by law.

In the event of a default by tenant, owner may elect to (a) continue the lease in effect and enforce all owner's rights and remedies hereunder, including the right to recover the rent as it becomes due, or (b) at any time, terminate all of tenant's rights hereunder and recover from tenant all damages owner may incur by reason of the breach of the lease, including the cost of recovering the premises, and including the worth at the time of such termination, or at the time of an award if suit be instituted to enforce this provision, of the amount by which the unpaid rent for the balance of the term exceeds the amount of such rental loss which the owner proves could reasonably be avoided.

Page 6 of 9

LEASE/RENTAL AND DEPOSIT RECEIPT - Continued

SECTION FIFTEEN - SECURITY- The security deposit set forth above, if any, shall secure the performance of tenant's obligations hereunder. Owner may, but shall not be obligated to, apply all or portions of said deposit on account of tenant's obligations hereunder. Any balance remaining upon termination shall be returned to tenant. Tenant shall not have the right to apply the security deposit in payment of the last month's rent.

SECTION SIXTEEN - DEPOSIT REFUNDS- The balance of all deposits shall be refunded within _____ weeks from date possession is delivered to owner,
       (number)
together with a statement showing any charges made against such deposits by owner.

SECTION SEVENTEEN - ATTORNEYS' FEES- In any legal action brought by either party to enforce the terms hereof or relating to the demised premises, the prevailing party shall be entitled to all costs incurred in connection with such action, including reasonable attorneys' fees.

SECTION EIGHTEEN - WAIVER- No failure of owner to enforce any term hereof shall be deemed a waiver, nor shall any acceptance of a partial payment of rent be deemed a waiver of owner's right to the full amount thereof.

SECTION NINETEEN - NOTICES- Any notice which either party may or is required to give, may be given by mailing the same, postage prepaid, to tenant at the premises or to owner at the address show below, or at such other places as may be designated by the parties from time to time.

LEASE/RENTAL AND DEPOSIT RECEIPT - Continued

SECTION TWENTY - HOLDING OVER-   Any holding over after expiration hereof, with the consent of owner, shall be construed as a month-to-month tenancy in accordance with the terms hereof, as applicable, until either party shall terminate the same by giving _____ days' written notice delivered by certified mail.
(number)

SECTION TWENTY-ONE - TIME   Time is of the essence of this agreement.

SECTION TWENTY-TWO - ADDITIONAL TERMS AND CONDITIONS-   Insert any additional terms and agreements which both parties may deem necessary or useful, mutually agreed upon, or, if none, cross out this paragraph. _____

_____

_____

_____

_____.

SECTION TWENTY-THREE - ENTIRE AGREEMENT-   The foregoing constitutes the entire agreement between the parties and may be modified only by a writing signed by both parties. The following exhibits, if any, have been made a part of this agreement before the parties' execution hereof: _____
(list exhibits or insert "none")

_____.

The undersigned tenant hereby acknowledges receipt of a copy hereof.

In witness whereof the parties have executed this agreement in the City of _____, State of _____, day and year first above written.

LEASE/RENTAL AND DEPOSIT RECEIPT - Continued

_____   _____
(Owner's signature)   (Tenant's signature)

_____   _____
(Owner's signature)   (Tenant's signature)

If required by state law, signatures of two witnesses for owner and two witnesses for tenant should sign this agreement.

_____   _____
(Witness for landlord)   (Witness for tenant)

_____   _____
(Witness for landlord)   (Witness for tenant)

SELLING REAL PROPERTY

I. PREPARING TO SELL

APPROXIMATE SELLER'S PROCEEDS: FOR SALE BY OWNER

_____
(Name(s) of seller)

_____
(Address of home to be sold)

_____
(City)

_____
(County)

_____
(State)

LISTED PRICE

    First trust deed _____

    Second trust deed _____

    Second trust deed _____

EQUITY _____

SELLING OBLIGATIONS:

    Title insurance _____

    Recordings _____

    Homeowner's warranty _____

    Taxes (current) _____

    Water & sewer escrow _____

    VA/FHA discount _____

    Interest on mortgage _____

    Prepayment penalty _____

TOTAL _____

APPROXIMATE SELLER'S PROCEEDS - Continued

EQUITY   _____

TOTAL OBLIGATIONS   _____

PROCEEDS   _____

Possible additional credits or debits:

        Proration of property tax

        Return of balance in escrow account

        Proration or cancellation of fire insurance

Seller is fully aware that this cost estimate has been prepared to assist in computing seller's costs. Whenever possible, the _maximum_ charges that can be expected have been used. Therefore, these figures cannot be guaranteed by seller or any of seller's representatives.

_____ have read the above figures and acknowledge receipt of a copy of
(I/we)
this form.

                                          _____
                                          (seller's signature)

                                          _____
                                          (seller's signature)

The approximate seller's proceeds calculated above will vary according to any differences in unpaid loan balances, escrows (if any), and any expenses for required corrective and/or preventive work.

REQUEST FOR LOAN INFORMATION

_____, 19___
(month and day)   (yr)

TO: _____
     (Name of lender)

     _____
     (Address)

     _____
     (City)

     _____
     (County)

     _____
     (State)

RE: Property located at _____
                         (Address)

                         _____
                         (City)

                         _____
                         (County)

                         _____
                         (State)

Lenders:

   I am the owner of the above property, which I am selling myself. In order to assist my sale of the property, I would appreciate the following information returned to me in the enclosed envelope with respect to the loan you are presently holding on my property.

Loan no. _____

Original amount of loan _____ Dollars ($_____)

   Present balance _____ Dollars ($_____)

Page 1 of 3

REQUEST FOR LOAN INFORMATION - Continued

As of _____, 19____ (date of last payment)
      (month and day)   (yr)

Type of loan (VA/FHA/Conv.) _____

Private mortgage insurance (if any) _____

Interest rate _____ %

    Is interest rate constant throughout the loan? _____ If no, please

    explain: _____

    _____.

Payment: P&I _____ Dollars ($_____)

    Taxes _____ Dollars ($_____)

    Insurance _____ Dollars ($_____)

Current escrow balance _____ Dollars ($_____)

    Is this included in the loan balance above? _____

Can loan be assumed at the present interest rate? _____

    If not, what will the interest rate be? _____

Assumption fee _____ Dollars ($_____)

    Other assumption charges (if any) _____ Dollars ($_____)

Must buyer qualify to assume loan? _____

Is interest in advance or arrears? _____

Prepayment penalty, if any (please explain) _____

_____

Do you have an improvement survey in your files? _____

What company issued the current title insurance policy? _____

    What is the date of said title insurance? _____

Page 2 of 3

REQUEST FOR LOAN INFORMATION - Continued

Except for increased rate and assumption fee information, it is understood that the above is subject to your issuance of an assumption or payoff statement, and is further subject to the current quality of the security and credit worthiness of a prospective purchaser. Should this property be sold on assumption terms, prior to closing the transaction, a formal assumption or payoff statement will be requested.

In the event the loan you are holding on the above described property is an FHA loan, in order to avoid an additional month's interest, please accept this as our written notice to prepay.

Thank you for your cooperation in this matter.

Sincerely,

_____
(Signature of owner)

_____
(Signature of owner)

_____
(Current address)

_____
(City)

_____
(County)

_____
(State)

REQUEST FOR LOAN INFORMATION: SHORT FORM

TO:

_____
(Name of lender)

_____
(Address)

_____
(City)

_____
(County)

_____
(State)

Please answer the following questions regarding the property at

_____
(Address)

_____
(City)

_____
(County)

_____
(State)

Loan no. _____

Original amount of loan _____

Date loan originated _____

Interest rate (current) _____

Type of loan (VA/FHA/Conv.) _____

Is loan assumable? _____

Mortgage company require approval for assumption? _____

Page 1 of 2

==

REQUEST FOR LOAN INFORMATION: SHORT FORM - Continued

Transfer fee _____

Prepayment penalty _____

Loan balance (current) _____

P.I.T.I. per month _____

Escrow balance (current) _____

Term of loan _____

Interest increase upon assumption? _____

If so, how much? _____

Date: _____, 19_____   BY: _____
     (month and day)   (yr)   (Name of owner)

                                              _____
                                              (Signature of owner)

                                              _____
                                              (Address)

                                              _____
                                              (City)

                                              _____
                                              (County)

                                              _____
                                              (State)

II. CONTRACTS

ASSUMPTION CONTRACT TO BUY AND SELL RESIDENTIAL REAL ESTATE

Agreement made _____, 19____, between:
_____(month and day)_____   _____(yr)_____

_____ and _____
(Name(s) of seller)   (Name(s) of purchaser)

herein referred to as seller, of   herein referred to as purchaser, of

_____   _____
(Address)   (Address)

_____   _____
(City)   (City)

_____   _____
(County)   (County)

_____   _____
(State)   (State)

RECITALS -

1. The undersigned seller hereby acknowledges having received from

_____
(name(s) of person(s) or entity providing earnest money)

the sum of _____ Dollars ($_____) in the form of
_____(amount of earnest money)_____

_____ to be held in a
(personal check/cashier's check/promissory note)

trust account at _____ Bank as earnest money and part
_____(name of bank)_____

payment for the following described real estate in

_____
(Town/township/city/or as case may be)

_____
(County)

_____
(State)

Page 1 of 11

CONTRACT: RESIDENTIAL REAL ESTATE - Continued

which is described as follows: _____
                                    (legal description)

_____,

together with all improvements thereon and all fixtures of a permanent nature

currently on the premises except as hereinafter provided, in their present

condition, ordinary wear and tear excepted, known as

_____
(Address)

_____
(City)

_____
(County)

_____
(State)

and hereinafter called the property.

2. The undersigned purchaser, _____,
                                (name(s) of purchaser as they wish to take title)

as _____ hereby agree to buy the property and the
   (joint tenants/tenants in common)

seller hereby agrees to sell the property upon the terms and conditions stated

herein:

SECTION ONE - PURCHASE PRICE AND TERMS OF PAYMENT- 1. The purchase price shall be

U.S. _____ Dollars ($_____), payable as
     (full amount of purchase price)

follows: _____ Dollars ($_____) hereby
         (amount of earnest money)

receipted for; the balance of the purchase price shall be payable in the following

manner in U.S. currency, certified or cashier's funds:

_____ Dollars ($_____),
(difference between purchase price & earnest money)

CONTRACT: RESIDENTIAL REAL ESTATE - Continued

to be paid by purchaser named herein assuming and agreeing to pay first mortgage loan now of record having an unpaid balance of approximately

_____ Dollars ($_____) as of _____,
                                                              (month and day)

19___, (the exact balance to be adjusted at time of closing) payable at the rate
   (yr)

of _____ Dollars ($_____) per month which includes

principal and interest at _____ per cent (_____%) per annum,

plus taxes and insurance; and the balance of the purchase price in cash at time of

delivery of deed.

2. Additional provisions are: (if none, insert "none other") _____

_____

_____

_____

_____

_____

_____

_____

_____.

3. Price to include any of the following items currently on the property:
lighting, heating, plumbing, ventilating, and central air conditioning fixtures,
attached TV antennas and/or water softener (if owned by seller); all outdoor
plants, window and porch shades, venetian blinds, storm windows, storm doors,
screens, curtain rods, drapery rods, attached mirrors, linoleum, floor tile,
awnings, fireplace screen and grate, built-in kitchen appliances, wall-to-wall

CONTRACT: RESIDENTIAL REAL ESTATE - Continued

carpeting and _____

(list any additional items to be included or insert "none other")

_____

_____

_____ ,

all in their present condition, conveyed free and clear of all taxes, liens and

encumbrances except as provided in SECTION TWO, Paragraph 1, provided, however,

that the following fixtures of a permanent nature are excluded from this sale:

_____

(list any exclusions of personal property, including preprinted items in Paragraph

_____

3 which seller intends to remove or insert "none other")

_____ .

Personal property shall be conveyed by bill of sale.

4. If a new loan is to be obtained by purchaser from a third party, purchaser

agrees to promptly and diligently (a) apply for such loan, (b) execute all

documents and furnish all information and documents required by the lender, and

(c) pay the customary costs of obtaining such loan. Then if such loan is not

approved on or before _____, 19___, or if so approved but is not

(month and day)   (yr)

available at time of closing, this contract shall be null and void and all

payments and things of value received hereunder shall be returned to purchaser.

5. If a note and trust deed or mortgage is to be assumed, purchaser agrees to

apply for a loan assumption if required and agrees to pay (1) a loan transfer fee

not to exceed _____ Dollars ($_____) and (2) an interest

rate not to exceed _____ per cent (_____%) per annum. If the

loan to be assumed has provisions for a shared equity or variable interest rates

Page 4 of 11

CONTRACT: RESIDENTIAL REAL ESTATE - Continued

or variable payments, this contract is conditioned upon the purchaser reviewing and consenting to such provisions. If the lender's consent to a loan assumption is required, this contract is conditioned upon obtaining such consent without change in the terms and conditions of such loan except as herein provided.

6. If a note is to be made payable to seller as partial or full payment of the purchase price, this contract shall not be assignable by purchaser without written consent of seller.

7. Cost of any appraisal for loan purposes to be obtained after this date shall be paid by _____.
   (purchaser or as case may be)

8. An abstract of title to the property, certified to date, or a current commitment for title insurance policy in an amount equal to the purchase price, at seller's option and expense, shall be furnished to purchaser on or before _____, 19____. If seller elects to furnish said title insurance
   (month and day)   (yr)
commitment, seller will deliver the title insurance policy to purchaser after closing and pay the premium thereon.

9. The date of closing shall be the date for delivery of deed as provided in SECTION TWO, Paragraph 1. The hour and place of closing shall be as designated by mutual consent.

SECTION TWO - TITLE-

1. Title shall be merchantable in seller, except as stated in this paragraph and in Paragraphs 2 and 3 of this Section. Subject to payment or tender as above provided and compliance by purchaser with the other terms and provisions hereof,

CONTRACT: RESIDENTIAL REAL ESTATE - Continued

seller shall execute and deliver a good and sufficient _____
                                                            (type of deed)

warranty deed to purchaser on _____, 19___, or, by mutual
                               (month and day)   (yr)

agreement, at an earlier date, conveying the property free and clear of all taxes,

except the general taxes for the year of closing, and except _____
                                                              (list any other taxes

such as personal property taxes, association fees and dues, water taxes or fees,

_____,

or insert "none other")

free and clear of all liens for special improvements installed as of the date of

purchaser's signature hereon, whether assessed or not; free and clear of all liens

and encumbrances except _____
                         (list any loans remaining after closing which are to be

assumed by purchaser or wrapped, or insert "none")

_____,

and except recorded and/or apparent easements for telephone, electricity, water,

sanitary sewer, and easements for _____
                                   (others such as right of way, shared wells,

septic tanks; or insert "none other")

_____;

and except the following restrictive covenants which do not contain a right of

reverter: _____
           (list any covenant or deed restriction or insert "none")

_____,

and subject to building and zoning regulations.

2. Except as stated in Paragraphs 1 and 3 of this Section, if title is not

merchantable and written notice of defect(s) is given by purchaser to seller on or

CONTRACT: RESIDENTIAL REAL ESTATE - Continued

before date of closing, seller shall use reasonable effort to correct such defect(s) prior to date of closing. If seller is unable to correct said defect(s) on or before date of closing, at seller's option and upon written notice to purchaser on or before date of closing, the date of closing shall be extended

_____ days for the purpose of correcting said defect(s). Except
(number)

as stated in Paragraph 3 of this Section, if title is not rendered merchantable as provided in this paragraph, at purchaser's option, this contract shall be void and of no effect and each party hereto shall be released from all obligations hereunder and all payments and things of value received hereunder shall be returned to purchaser.

3. If the total indebtedness secured by liens on the property exceeds the purchase price, this contract shall be void and of no effect and each party hereto shall be released from all obligations hereunder and all payments and things of value received hereunder shall be returned to purchaser.

SECTION THREE - TAXES- General taxes for the year of closing, based on the most recent levy and the most recent assessment, prepaid rents, water rents, sewer rents, FHA mortgage insurance premiums and interest on encumbrances, if any and

_____
(list other items remaining on property which will be pro-rated between purchaser

_____
and seller at closing; or insert "none")

_____

shall be apportioned to date of delivery of deed.

SECTION FOUR - POSSESSION OF PROPERTY AND RESPONSIBILITIES- Possession of the property shall be delivered to purchaser (check and complete one of the following options):

CONTRACT: RESIDENTIAL REAL ESTATE - Continued

a) _____ on the date of delivery of deed (if property is vacant);

OR

b) _____ on or before _____ days after delivery of deed (if
(number)

property is to be vacated by owner prior to closing);

OR

c) _____ on the date of delivery subject to a _____
(period of time)

term lease or rental agreement with _____
(name(s) of tenant(s))

as tenant(s), which shall be assigned to purchaser at closing and which

expires on _____, 19___ (if property is rented and
(month and day)   (yr)

tenants, by mutual agreement of purchaser and seller, will remain as

tenants after closing).

If seller fails to deliver possession on the date herein specified, seller

shall be subject to eviction and shall be liable for a daily rental of

_____ Dollars ($_____) until possession is delivered.

SECTION FIVE - DESTRUCTION OF PREMISES-   In the event that the property is

damaged by fire or other casualty prior to the time of closing in an amount of not

more than ten percent of the total purchase price, seller shall be obligated to

repair the same before the date herein provided for delivery of deed. In the

event such damage cannot be repaired within said time or if damage shall exceed

such sum, this contract may be cancelled at the option of the purchaser and all

payments and things of value received hereunder shall be returned to purchaser.

Should the purchaser elect to carry out this agreement despite such damage,

purchaser shall be entitled to all the credit for the insurance proceeds resulting

CONTRACT: RESIDENTIAL REAL ESTATE - Continued

from such damage not exceeding, however, the purchase price. Should any fixtures or services fail between the date of this contract and the date of possession or the date of delivery of deed, whichever shall be earlier, then the seller shall be liable for the repair or replacement of such fixtures or services with a unit of similar size, age and quality, or an equivalent credit.

SECTION SIX - TIME OF ESSENCE; DEFAULT- Time is of the essence hereof. If any note or check received as earnest money hereunder or any other payment due hereunder is not paid, honored or tendered when due, or if any other obligation hereunder is not performed as herein provided, there shall be the following remedies:

1. **IF SELLER IS IN DEFAULT,** (a) purchaser may elect to treat this contract as terminated, in which case all payments and things of value received hereunder shall be returned to purchaser and purchaser may recover such damages as may be proper, or (b) purchaser may elect to treat this contract as being in full force and effect and purchaser shall have the right to an action for specific performance or damages or both.

2. **IF PURCHASER IS IN DEFAULT,** then all payments and things of value received hereunder shall be forfeited by purchaser and retained on behalf of seller and both parties shall thereafter be released from all obligations hereunder. It is agreed that such payments and things of value are **liquidated damages** and (except as provided in Paragraph 3 of this Section) are the **seller's sole and only remedy** for the purchaser's failure to perform the obligations of this contract. Seller expressly waives the remedies of specific performance and additional damages.

CONTRACT: RESIDENTIAL REAL ESTATE - Continued

SECTION SEVEN - ATTORNEYS' FEES- Anything to the contrary herein notwithstanding, in the event of any litigation arising out of this contract, the court may award to the prevailing party all reasonable costs and expenses, including attorneys' fees.

SECTION EIGHT - ADDITIONAL PROVISIONS- _____
(insert any added provisions or

_____
contingencies not included above or insert "none")

_____

_____

_____

_____

_____

_____

_____

_____

SECTION NINE - CAPTIONS- The captions used herein are merely for easy reference and shall have no effect on the agreement or the terms and conditions herein contained.

SECTION TEN - BINDING EFFECT OF CONTRACT- If this proposal is accepted by seller in writing and purchaser receives notice of such acceptance on or before _____ o'clock _____.m., _____, 19____, this
                                                    (month and day)   (yr)
instrument shall become a contract between seller and purchaser and shall inure to the benefit of the heirs, successors and assigns of such parties, except as stated in SECTION ONE, Paragraph 6.

Page 10 of 11

CONTRACT: RESIDENTIAL REAL ESTATE - Continued

_____
(Purchaser's signature)   (Date)

_____
(Address)

_____
(City)

_____
(County)

_____.
(State)

_____
(Purchaser's signature)   (Date)

_____
(Address)

_____
(City)

_____
(County)

_____.
(State)

THE FOLLOWING SECTION IS TO BE COMPLETED BY SELLER:

_____
(Seller's signature)   (Date)

_____
(Address)

_____
(City)

_____
(County)

_____.
(State)

_____
(Seller's signature)   (Date)

_____
(Address)

_____
(City)

_____
(County)

_____.
(State)

CONTRACT TO BUY AND SELL RESIDENTIAL REAL ESTATE: CASH TERMS

Agreement made _____ , 19____ , between:
            (month and day)   (yr)

_____   and   _____
(Name(s) of seller)   (Name(s) of purchaser)

herein referred to as seller, of   herein referred to as purchaser, of

_____   _____
(Address)   (Address)

_____   _____
(City)   (City)

_____   _____
(County)   (County)

_____   _____
(State)   (State)

RECITALS -

1. The undersigned seller hereby acknowledges having received from

_____
(name(s) of person(s) or entity providing earnest money)

the sum of _____ Dollars ($_____) in the form of
              (amount of earnest money)

_____ to be held in a
(personal check/cashier's check/promissory note)

trust account at _____ Bank as earnest money and part
               (name of bank)

payment for the following described real estate in

_____
(Town/township/city/or as case may be)

_____
(County)

_____
(State)

Page 1 of 10

CONTRACT FOR RESIDENTIAL REAL ESTATE: CASH TERMS - Continued

which is more particularly described as follows: _____
                                                              (legal description)

_____,

together with all improvements thereon and all fixtures of a permanent nature

currently on the premises except as hereinafter provided, in their present

condition, ordinary wear and tear excepted, known as

                            _____
                            (Address)

                            _____
                            (City)

                            _____
                            (County)

                            _____
                            (State)

and hereinafter called the property.

2. The undersigned purchaser, _____,
                                (name of purchaser(s) as they wish to take title)

as _____ hereby agree to buy the property and the
   (joint tenants/tenants in common)

seller hereby agrees to sell the property upon the terms and conditions stated

herein:

SECTION ONE - PURCHASE PRICE AND TERMS OF PAYMENT- 1. The purchase price shall be

U.S. _____ Dollars ($_____), payable as
     (full amount of purchase price)

follows: _____ Dollars ($_____) hereby
          (amount of earnest money)

receipted for; the balance of the purchase price shall be payable in the following

manner in U.S. currency, certified or cashier's funds: _____
                                                        (describe method of payment)

_____

_____

CONTRACT FOR RESIDENTIAL REAL ESTATE: CASH TERMS - Continued

_____

_____

_____ .

2.   Price to include any of the following items currently on the property:

lighting, heating, plumbing, ventilating, and central air conditioning fixtures,

attached TV antennas and/or water softener (if owned by seller); all outdoor

plants, window and porch shades, venetian blinds, storm windows, storm doors,

screens, curtain rods, drapery rods, attached mirrors, linoleum, floor tile,

awnings, fireplace screen and grate, built-in kitchen appliances, wall-to-wall

carpeting and _____

(list any additional items to be included or insert "none other")

_____

_____

_____ ,

all in their present condition, conveyed free and clear of all taxes, liens and

encumbrances except as provided in SECTION TWO, Paragraph 1, provided, however,

that the following fixtures of a permanent nature are excluded from this sale:

_____

(list any exclusions of personal property, including preprinted items in Paragraph

_____

2 which seller intends to remove or insert "none other")

_____ .

Personal property shall be conveyed by bill of sale.

3.   If a note is to be made payable to seller as partial or full payment of the

purchase price, this contract shall not be assignable by purchaser without written

consent of seller.

CONTRACT FOR RESIDENTIAL REAL ESTATE: CASH TERMS - Continued

4. Cost of any appraisal for loan purposes to be obtained after this date shall

be paid by _____ .
       (purchaser or as case may be)

5. An abstract of title to the property, certified to date, or a current

commitment for title insurance policy in an amount equal to the purchase price,

at seller's option and expense, shall be furnished to purchaser on or before

_____ , 19____ .   If seller elects to furnish said title insurance
(month and day)   (yr)

commitment, seller will deliver the title insurance policy to purchaser after

closing and pay the premium thereon.

6. The date of closing shall be the date for delivery of deed as provided in

SECTION TWO, Paragraph 1. The hour and place of closing shall be as designated by

mutual consent.

SECTION TWO - TITLE-

1. Title shall be merchantable in seller, except as stated in this paragraph and

in Paragraphs 2 and 3 of this Section. Subject to payment or tender as above

provided and compliance by purchaser with the other terms and provisions hereof,

seller shall execute and deliver a good and sufficient _____
                                                              (type of deed)

warranty deed to purchaser on _____ , 19____ , or, by mutual
                                   (month and day)   (yr)

agreement, at an earlier date, conveying the property free and clear of all taxes,

except the general taxes for the year of closing, and except _____
                                                                  (list any other taxes

_____
such as personal property taxes, association fees or dues, water taxes or fees or

_____ and free and clear of all liens
insert "none other")

Page 4 of 10

CONTRACT FOR RESIDENTIAL REAL ESTATE: CASH TERMS - Continued

for special improvements installed as of the date of purchaser's signature hereon, whether assessed or not; free and clear of all liens and encumbrances except

_____

(list any loans remaining after closing which are to be assumed by purchaser or

_____

wrapped or insert "none other")

and except recorded and/or apparent easements for telephone, electricity, water,

sanitary sewer, and easements for _____

                       (others such as right of way, shared wells,

_____

driveways, septic tanks; or insert "none other")

and except the following restrictive covenants which do not contain a right of

reverter: _____

        (list any covenant or deed restriction or insert "none")

_____,

and subject to building and zoning regulations.

2. Except as stated in Paragraphs 1 and 3 of this Section, if title is not merchantable and written notice of defect(s) is given by purchaser to seller on or before date of closing, seller shall use reasonable effort to correct such defect(s) prior to date of closing. If seller is unable to correct said defect(s) on or before date of closing, at seller's option and upon written notice to purchaser on or before date of closing, the date of closing shall be extended

_____ days for the purpose of correcting said defect(s). Except
(number)

as noted in Paragraph 3 of this Section, if title is not rendered merchantable as provided in this paragraph, at purchaser's option, this contract shall be void and of no effect and each party hereto shall be released from all obligations hereunder and all payments and things of value received hereunder shall be returned to purchaser.

CONTRACT FOR RESIDENTIAL REAL ESTATE: CASH TERMS - Continued

3. If the total indebtedness secured by liens on the property exceeds the purchase price, this contract shall be void and of no effect and each party hereto shall be released from all obligations hereunder and all payments and things of value received hereunder shall be returned to purchaser.

SECTION THREE - TAXES- General taxes for the year of closing, based on the most recent levy and the most recent assessment, prepaid rents, water rents, sewer rents, FHA mortgage insurance premiums and interest on encumbrances, if any and

_____

(list other items remaining on property which will be pro-rated between purchaser

_____

and seller at closing; or insert "none")

_____

shall be apportioned to date of delivery of deed.

SECTION FOUR - POSSESSION OF PROPERTY AND RESPONSIBILITIES- Possession of the property shall be delivered to purchaser (check and complete one of the following options):

    a) _____ on the date of delivery of deed (if property is vacant);

OR

    b) _____ on or before _____ days after delivery of deed (if
                               (number)

       property is to be vacated by owner prior to closing);

OR

    c) _____ on the date of delivery subject to a _____
                                      (period of time)

       term lease or rental agreement with _____
                                    (name(s) of tenant(s))

Page 6 of 10

CONTRACT FOR RESIDENTIAL REAL ESTATE: CASH TERMS - Continued

as tenant(s), which shall be assigned to purchaser at closing and which

expires on _____ , 19____ (if property is rented and
             (month and day)   (yr)

tenants, by mutual agreement of purchaser and seller, will remain as

tenants after closing).

    If seller fails to deliver possession on the date herein specified, seller

shall be subject to eviction and shall be liable for a daily rental of

_____ Dollars ($_____) until possession is delivered.

SECTION FIVE - DESTRUCTION OF PREMISES- In the event that the property is damaged by fire or other casualty prior to the time of closing in an amount of not more than ten percent of the total purchase price, seller shall be obligated to repair the same before the date herein provided for delivery of deed. In the event such damage cannot be repaired within said time or if damage shall exceed such sum, this contract may be terminated at the option of the purchaser and all payments and things of value received hereunder shall be returned to purchaser. Should the purchaser elect to carry out this agreement despite such damage, purchaser shall be entitled to all the credit for the insurance proceeds resulting from such damage not exceeding, however, the total purchase price. Should any fixtures or services fail between the date of this agreement and the date of possession or the date of delivery of deed, whichever shall be earlier, then the seller shall be liable for the repair or replacement of such fixtures or services with a unit of similar size, age and quality, or an equivalent credit.

SECTION SIX - TIME OF ESSENCE; DEFAULT- Time is of the essence hereof. If any note or check received as earnest money hereunder or any other payment due hereunder is not paid, honored or tendered when due, or if any other obligation

CONTRACT FOR RESIDENTIAL REAL ESTATE: CASH TERMS - Continued

hereunder is not performed as herein provided, there shall be the following remedies:

1. **IF SELLER IS IN DEFAULT,** (a) purchaser may elect to treat this contract as terminated, in which case all payments and things of value received hereunder shall be returned to purchaser and purchaser may recover such damages as may be proper, or (b) purchaser may elect to treat this contract as being in full force and effect and purchaser shall have the right to an action for specific performance or damages or both.

2. **IF PURCHASER IS IN DEFAULT,** then all payments and things of value received hereunder shall be forfeited by purchaser and retained on behalf of seller and both parties shall thereafter be released from all obligations hereunder. It is agreed that such payments and things of value are **liquidated damages** and (except as provided in Paragraph 3 of this Section) are the **seller's sole and only remedy** for the purchaser's failure to perform the obligations of this contract. Seller expressly waives the remedies of specific performance and additional damages.

SECTION SEVEN - ATTORNEYS' FEES- Anything to the contrary herein notwithstanding, in the event of any litigation arising out of this contract, the court may award to the prevailing party all reasonable costs and expenses, including attorneys' fees.

SECTION EIGHT - ADDITIONAL PROVISIONS- _____
(insert any added provisions or

_____
contingencies not included above or insert "none")

_____

_____

Page 8 of 10

CONTRACT FOR RESIDENTIAL REAL ESTATE: CASH TERMS - Continued

_____

_____

_____

_____.

_____

_____

 . _____

_____

SECTION NINE - CAPTIONS- the captions used herein are merely for easy reference and shall have no effect on the agreement or the terms and conditions herein contained.

SECTION TEN - BINDING EFFECT OF CONTRACT- If this proposal is accepted by seller in writing and purchaser receives notice of such acceptance on or before

_____ o'clock _____.m., _____, 19___, this
                                             (month and day)   (yr)

instrument shall become a contract between seller and purchaser and shall inure to the benefit of the heirs, successors and assigns of such parties, except as stated in SECTION ONE, Paragraph 6.

_____   _____
(Purchaser's signature)   (Date)   (Purchaser's signature)   (Date)

_____   _____
(Address)   (Address)

_____   _____
(City)   (City)

_____   _____
(County)   (County)

_____.   _____.
(State)   (State)

Page 9 of 10

CONTRACT FOR RESIDENTIAL REAL ESTATE: CASH TERMS - Continued

THE FOLLOWING SECTION IS TO BE COMPLETED BY SELLER:

_____   _____
(Seller's signature)   (Date)

_____
(Address)

_____
(City)

_____
(County)

_____.
(State)

_____   _____
(Seller's signature)   (Date)

_____
(Address)

_____
(City)

_____
(County)

_____.
(State)

Page 10 of 10

**CONTRACT TO BUY AND SELL RESIDENTIAL REAL ESTATE
WITH PROVISIONS FOR CONVENTIONAL, FHA OR VA LOAN**

Agreement made _____, 19____, between:
(month and day)   (yr)

_____ and _____
(Name(s) of seller)   (Name(s) of purchaser)

herein referred to as seller, of   herein referred to as purchaser, of

_____   _____
(Address)   (Address)

_____   _____
(City)   (City)

_____   _____
(County)   (County)

_____   _____
(State)   (State)

RECITALS -

1. The undersigned seller hereby acknowledges having received from

_____
(name(s) of person(s) or entity providing earnest money)

the sum of _____ Dollars ($_____) in the form of
(amount of earnest money)

_____ to be held in a
(personal check/cashier's check/promissory note)

trust account at _____ Bank as earnest money and part
(name of bank)

payment for the following described real estate in

_____
(Town/township/city/or as case may be)

_____
(County)

_____
(State)

RESIDENTIAL REAL ESTATE CONTRACT: 3 LOAN OPTIONS - Continued

which is described as follows: _____
(legal description of real estate)

_____,

together with all improvements thereon and all fixtures of a permanent nature

currently on the premises except as hereinafter provided, in their present

condition, ordinary wear and tear excepted, known as

_____
(Address)

_____
(City)

_____
(County)

_____
(State)

and hereinafter called the property.

2.   Subject to the provisions of SECTION SIX, the undersigned purchaser,

_____, as
(name of purchaser(s) as they wish to take title)

_____ hereby agree to buy the property
(joint tenants/tenants in common)

and the seller hereby agrees to sell the property upon the terms and conditions

stated herein:

SECTION ONE - PURCHASE PRICE AND TERMS OF PAYMENT-   The purchase price shall be

1.   U.S. _____ Dollars ($_____), payable as
(full amount of purchase price)

follows: _____ Dollars ($_____) hereby
(amount of earnest money)

receipted for; _____Dollars
(difference between purchase price & earnest money)

($_____) upon delivery of deed as follows: _____

Page 2 of 12

RESIDENTIAL REAL ESTATE CONTRACT: 3 LOAN OPTIONS - Continued

Dollars ($_____) additional cash or certified funds, plus a new first

loan (Check loan to be used: Conv _____ FHA _____ VA _____) of

_____ Dollars ($_____) to be amortized over a

period of _____ years, with monthly interest not to exceed
        (number)

_____ per cent (_____%) per annum with monthly principal and

interest payments of approximately _____ Dollars ($_____)

plus a monthly escrow deposit for taxes and insurance and _____ per

cent (_____%) mortgage insurance, if applicable. If FHA or VA loan, see the

provisions in the Addendum herein. Pursuant to Paragraph 3, purchaser agrees to

make loan application within _____ calendar days after notice of
                            (number)

acceptance of this contract, and agrees to pay loan service/origination fees not

to exceed _____ per cent (_____%) of the loan amount.

Seller agrees to pay a loan discount fee to lender not to exceed _____

per cent (_____%) of purchaser's loan amount.

2. Price to include any of the following items currently on the property:

lighting, heating, plumbing, ventilating, and central air conditioning fixtures,

attached TV antennas and/or water softener (if owned by seller); all outdoor

plants, window and porch shades, venetian blinds, storm windows, storm doors,

screens, curtain rods, drapery rods, attached mirrors, linoleum, floor tile,

awnings, fireplace screen and grate, built-in kitchen appliances, wall-to-wall

carpeting and _____
                (list any additional items of personal property to be included or

_____
insert "none other")

_____

_____,

RESIDENTIAL REAL ESTATE CONTRACT: 3 LOAN OPTIONS - Continued

all in their present condition, conveyed free and clear of all taxes, liens and encumbrances except as provided in SECTION TWO, Paragraph 1, provided, however, that the following fixtures of a permanent nature are excluded form this sale:

_____

(list any exclusions of personal property, including preprinted items in Paragraph

_____

2 which seller intends to remove or insert "none")

_____.

Personal property shall be conveyed by bill of sale.

3. If a new loan is to be obtained by purchaser from a third party, purchaser agrees to promptly and diligently (a) apply for such loan, (b) execute all documents and furnish all information and documents required by the lender, and (c) pay the customary costs of obtaining such loan. Then if such loan is not approved on or before _____, 19____, or if so approved but is not

                              (month and day)   (yr)

available at time of closing, this contract shall be null and void and all payments and things of value received hereunder shall be returned to purchaser.

4. If a note and trust deed or mortgage is to be assumed, purchaser agrees to apply for a loan assumption if required and agrees to pay (1) a loan transfer fee not to exceed _____ Dollars ($_____) and (2) an interest rate not to exceed _____ per cent (_____%) per annum. If the loan to be assumed has provisions for a shared equity or variable interest rates or variable payments, this contract is conditioned upon the purchaser reviewing and consenting to such provisions. If the lender's consent to a loan assumption is required, this contract is conditioned upon obtaining such consent without change in the terms and conditions of such loan except as herein provided.

Page 4 of 12

RESIDENTIAL REAL ESTATE CONTRACT: 3 LOAN OPTIONS - Continued

5. If a note is to be made payable to seller as partial or full payment of the purchase price, this contract shall not be assignable by purchaser without written consent of seller.

6. Cost of any appraisal for loan purposes to be obtained after this date shall be paid by _____.
    (purchaser or as case may be)

7. An abstract of title to the property, certified to date, or a current commitment for title insurance policy in an amount equal to the purchase price, at seller's option and expense, shall be furnished to purchaser on or before

    _____, 19___. If seller elects to furnish said title insurance
    (month and day)   (yr)

    commitment, seller will deliver the title insurance policy to purchaser after closing and pay the premium thereon.

8. The date of closing shall be the date for delivery of deed as provided in SECTION TWO, Paragraph 1. The hour and place of closing shall be as designated by mutual consent.

SECTION TWO - TITLE-

1. Title shall be merchantable in seller, except as stated in this paragraph and paragraphs 2 and 3 of this Section. Subject to payment or tender as above provided and compliance by purchaser with the other terms and provisions hereof, seller shall execute and deliver a good and sufficient _____
    (type of deed)

    warranty deed to purchaser on _____, 19___, or, by mutual
    (month and day)   (yr)

    agreement, at an earlier date, conveying the property free and clear of all taxes, except the general taxes for the year of closing, and except _____

RESIDENTIAL REAL ESTATE CONTRACT: 3 LOAN OPTIONS - Continued

(list any other taxes other than general, such as personal property taxes on

income property, association fees or dues, water taxes or fees or insert "none")

free and clear of all liens for special improvements installed as of the date of

purchaser's signature hereon, whether assessed or not; free and clear of all liens

and encumbrances except _____
                        (list any loans remaining after closing which are to be

_____

assumed by purchaser or wrapped, or insert "none")

_____,

and except recorded and/or apparent easements for telephone, electricity, water,

sanitary sewer, and easements for _____
                                 (list other easements such as right of way,

_____

shared wells, septic tanks, driveways, or insert "none other")

_____;

and except the following restrictive covenants which do not contain a right of

reverter: _____
         (list any covenant or deed restriction or insert "none")

_____,

and subject to building and zoning regulations.

2. Except as stated in Paragraphs 1 and 3 of this Section, if title is not

merchantable and written notice of defect(s) is given by purchaser to seller on or

before date of closing, seller shall use reasonable effort to correct such

defect(s) prior to date of closing. If seller is unable to correct said defect(s)

on or before date of closing, at seller's option and upon written notice to

purchaser on or before date of closing, the date of closing shall be extended

_____ days for the purpose of correcting said defect(s). Except
(number)

Page 6 of 12

RESIDENTIAL REAL ESTATE CONTRACT: 3 LOAN OPTIONS - Continued

as stated in Paragraph 3 of this Section, if title is not rendered merchantable as provided in this Paragraph 2, at purchaser's option, this contract shall be void and of no effect and each party hereto shall be released from all obligations hereunder and all payments and things of value received hereunder shall be returned to purchaser.

3. If the total indebtedness secured by liens on the property exceeds the purchase price, this contract shall be void and of no effect and each party hereto shall be released from all obligations hereunder and all payments and things of value received hereunder shall be returned to purchaser.

SECTION THREE - TAXES- General taxes for the year of closing, based on the most recent levy and the most recent assessment, prepaid rents, water rents, sewer rents, FHA mortgage insurance premiums and interest on encumbrances, if any and

_____
(list other items remaining on property which will be pro-rated between purchaser

_____
and seller at closing; or insert "none")

_____

shall be apportioned to date of delivery of deed.

SECTION FOUR - POSSESSION OF PROPERTY AND RESPONSIBILITIES- Possession of the property shall be delivered to purchaser (check and complete one of the following options):

    a) _____ on the date of delivery of deed (if property is vacant);

OR

    b) _____ on or before _____ days after delivery of deed (if
                          (number)

    property is to be vacated by owner prior to closing);

OR

RESIDENTIAL REAL ESTATE CONTRACT: 3 LOAN OPTIONS - Continued

c) _____ on the date of delivery subject to a _____
                                              (period of time)

term lease or rental agreement with _____
                                    (name(s) of tenant(s))

as tenant(s), which shall be assigned to purchaser at closing and which

expires on _____, 19____ (if property is rented and
           (month and day)   (yr)

tenants, by mutual agreement of purchaser and seller, will remain as

tenants after closing).

If seller fails to deliver possession on the date herein specified, seller

shall be subject to eviction and shall be liable for a daily rental of

_____ Dollars ($_____) until possession is delivered.

SECTION FIVE - DESTRUCTION OF PREMISES- In the event that the property is damaged
by fire or other casualty prior to the time of closing in an amount of not more
than ten percent of the total purchase price, seller shall be obligated to repair
the same before the date herein provided for delivery of deed. In the event such
damage cannot be repaired within said time or if damage shall exceed such sum,
this contract may be terminated at the option of the purchaser and all payments
and things of value received hereunder shall be returned to purchser. Should the
purchaser elect to carry out this agreement despite such damage, purchaser shall
be entitled to all the credit for the insurance proceeds resulting from such
damage not exceeding, however, the total purchase price. Should any fixtures or
services fail between the date of this agreement and the date of possession or the
date of delivery of deed, whichever shall be earlier, then the seller shall be
liable for the repair or replacement of such fixtures or services with a unit of
similar size, age and quality, or an equivalent credit.

RESIDENTIAL REAL ESTATE CONTRACT: 3 LOAN OPTIONS - Continued

SECTION SIX - TIME OF ESSENCE; DEFAULT- Time is of the essence hereof. If any note or check received as earnest money hereunder or any other payment due hereunder is not paid, honored or tendered when due, or if any other obligation hereunder is not performed as herein provided, there shall be the following remedies:

1. **IF SELLER IS IN DEFAULT,** (a) purchaser may elect to treat this contract as terminated, in which case all payments and things of value received hereunder shall be returned to purchaser and purchaser may recover such damages as may be proper, or (b) purchaser may elect to treat this contract as being in full force and effect and purchaser shall have the right to an action for specific performance or damages or both.

2. **IF PURCHASER IS IN DEFAULT,** then all payments and things of value received hereunder shall be forfeited by purchaser and retained on behalf of seller and both parties shall thereafter be released from all obligations hereunder. It is agreed that such payments and things of value are **liquidated damages** and (except as provided in Paragraph 3 of this Section) are the **seller's sole and only remedy** for the purchaser's failure to perform the obligations of this contract. Seller expressly waives the remedies of specific performance and additional damages.

SECTION SEVEN - ATTORNEYS' FEES- Anything to the contrary herein notwithstanding, in the event of any litigation arising out of this contract, the court may award to the prevailing party all reasonable costs and expenses, including attorneys' fees.

SECTION EIGHT - ADDITIONAL PROVISIONS- If performance is delayed by the lender under this agreement, the time for closing shall be once extended _____
                                                                      (number)

RESIDENTIAL REAL ESTATE CONTRACT: 3 LOAN OPTIONS - Continued

business days beyond the time stated in SECTION TWO, Paragraph 1. In addition,

(insert any added provisions or contingencies not included above or insert "none")

_____

_____

_____

_____

_____

_____

_____

_____

_____ .

SECTION NINE - CAPTIONS-   The captions used herein are merely for easy reference and shall have no effect on the agreement or the terms and conditions herein contained.

SECTION TEN - BINDING EFFECT OF CONTRACT- If this proposal is accepted by seller in writing and purchaser receives notice of such acceptance on or before

_____ o'clock _____ .m., _____ , 19 ____ , this
                                             (month and day)   (yr)

instrument shall become a contract between seller and purchaser and shall inure to the benefit of the heirs, successors and assigns of such parties, except as stated in SECTION ONE, Paragraph 6.

_____   _____
(Purchaser's signature)   (Date)   (Purchaser's signature)   (Date)

RESIDENTIAL REAL ESTATE CONTRACT: 3 LOAN OPTIONS - Continued

_____   _____
(Address)   (Address)

_____   _____
(City)   (City)

_____   _____
(County)   (County)

_____.   _____.
(State)   (State)

THE FOLLOWING SECTION IS TO BE COMPLETED BY SELLER:

    Seller accepts the above proposal this _____ day of
                                                  (number)

_____, 19____.
(month)   (yr)

_____   _____
(Seller's signature) (Date)   (Seller's signature) (Date)

_____   _____
(Address)   (Address)

_____   _____
(City)   (City)

_____   _____
(County)   (County)

_____.   _____.
(State)   (State)

ADDENDUM -

_____ IF A VA LOAN - It is expressly agreed that, notwithstanding any other provision of this sales agreement/contract, the veteran/purchaser shall not incur any penalty by forfeiture of earnest money or otherwise be obligated to complete the purchase of the property described herein if the contract purchase price or cost exceeds the reasonable value of the property established by the Veterans Administration. The veteran/purchaser shall, however, have the privilege and option of proceeding with the consumation of the contract without regard to the amount of the reasonable value established by the Veterans Administration.

Page 11 of 12

RESIDENTIAL REAL ESTATE CONTRACT: 3 LOAN OPTIONS - Continued

_____ IF AN FHA LOAN - It is expressly agreed that, notwithstanding any other provision of this contract, the purchaser shall not be obligated to complete the purchase of the property described herein or to incur any penalty by forfeiture of earnest money deposits or otherwise unless the seller has delivered to the purchaser a written statement issued by the Federal Housing Commissioner setting forth the appraised value of the property (excluding closing costs) of not less than _____ Dollars ($_____), which statement the seller hereby agrees to deliver to the purchaser promptly after such appraised value is made available to the seller. The purchaser shall, however, have the privilege and option of proceeding with the consumation of the contract without regard to the amount of the appraised valuation made by the Federal Housing Commissioner. The appraised valuation is arrived at to determine the maximum mortgage the Department of Housing and Urban Development will insure. HUD does not warrant the value or condition of the property. The purchaser should be satisfied that the price and the condition of the property are acceptable.

AND

_____ NO SIDE AGREEMENT (FHA) - We the undersigned, the seller(s) and purchaser(s) involved in this transaction each certify that the terms of the contract for the purchase are true, and that there are no other agreements entered into by any of these parties in connection with this transaction that are not attached to the sales agreement, to their best knowledge and belief. Purchaser(s) acknowledge(s) that the premises will be occupied as their primary residence.

| (Seller's Signature) | (Date) | (Purchaser's Signature) | (Date) |

| (Seller's Signature) | (Date) | (Purchaser's Signature) | (Date) |

CONTRACT TO BUY AND SELL REAL ESTATE: RESIDENTIAL CONDOMINIUM

Agreement made _____, 19____, between:
　　　　　　　　　　(month and day)　　　　　　　　　(yr)

_____　and　_____
(Name(s) of seller)　　　　　　　　　　　　　(Name(s) of purchaser)

herein referred to as seller, of　　　　herein referred to as purchaser, of

_____　　　_____
(Address)　　　　　　　　　　　　　　　　(Address)

_____　　　_____
(City)　　　　　　　　　　　　　　　　　(City)

_____　　　_____
(County)　　　　　　　　　　　　　　　(County)

_____　　　_____
(State)　　　　　　　　　　　　　　　　(State)

RECITALS -

1. The undersigned seller hereby acknowledges having received from

_____
(name(s) of person(s) or entity providing earnest money)

the sum of _____ Dollars ($_____) in the form of
　　　　　　(amount of earnest money)

_____ to be held in a
(personal check/cashier's check/promissory note)

trust account at _____ Bank as earnest money and part
　　　　　　　　　(name of bank)

payment for the following described real estate in

_____
(Town/township/city/or as case may be)

_____
(County)

_____
(State)

NOTE: This form may also be used for the sale of townhouses, planned unit developments and other residential building groups involving ownership of common elements.

CONTRACT FOR RESIDENTIAL CONDOMINIUM - Continued

which is described as follows: _____
(unit and building numbers with legal description)

_____ ,

according to the map or plat and declaration thereof recorded in said county

records, together with the interests, easements, rights and benefits appurtenant

to the ownership of such unit and together with all appurtenant improvements

thereon and all fixtures of a permanent nature currently on the premises except as

hereinafter provided, in their present condition, ordinary wear and tear excepted,

known as

Unit No. _____

Building No. _____

_____
(Address)

_____
(City)

_____
(County)

_____
(State)

and hereinafter called the property.

2.   Subject to the provisions of SECTION FIVE, the undersigned purchaser,

_____ , as
(name(s) of purchaser(s) as they wish to take title)

_____ hereby agrees to buy the property and the
(joint tenants/tenants in common)

seller hereby agrees to sell the property upon the terms and conditions stated

herein:

SECTION ONE - PURCHASE PRICE AND TERMS OF PAYMENT-

1.   The purchase price shall be U.S. _____ Dollars
(full amount of purchase price)

CONTRACT FOR RESIDENTIAL CONDOMINIUM - Continued

($_____), payable as follows: _____ Dollars
                                  (amount of earnest money)

($_____) hereby receipted for; the balance of the purchase price shall be

payable in the following manner in U.S. currency, certified or cashier's funds:

_____

_____

_____

_____

_____ .

2. Price to include any of the following items currently in said unit: lighting,
heating, plumbing, ventilating, and central air conditioning fixtures, attached TV
antennas and/or water softener (if owned by seller); all outdoor plants, window
and porch shades, venetian blinds, storm windows, storm doors, screens, curtain
rods, drapery rods, attached mirrors, linoleum, floor tile, awnings, fireplace
screen and grate, built-in kitchen appliances, wall-to-wall carpeting and

_____
(list any additional items of personal property to be included or insert "none")

_____

_____ ,

all in their present condition, conveyed free and clear of all taxes, liens and
encumbrances except as provided in SECTION TWO, Paragraph 1. Price shall also
include the use of the following parking facility or facilities: _____

_____ ;
(specify identification numbers of parking stalls or garages)
and the following storage facility or facilities: _____
                                    (specify identification

_____ .
numbers of storage areas)

Page 3 of 13

CONTRACT FOR RESIDENTIAL CONDOMINIUM - Continued

The following fixtures of a permanent nature are excluded from this sale:

_____

(list any exclusions of personal property, including preprinted items in Paragraph

_____

2 which seller intends to remove)

_____,

Personal property shall be conveyed by bill of sale.

3. If a new loan is to be obtained by purchaser from a third party, purchaser
agrees to promptly and diligently (a) apply for such loan, (b) execute all
documents and furnish all information and documents required by the lender, and
(c) pay the customary costs of obtaining such loan. Then if such loan is not
approved on or before _____, 19____, or if so approved but is not
                        (month and day)   (yr)
available at time of closing, this contract shall be null and void and all
payments and things of value received hereunder shall be returned to purchaser.

4. If a note and trust deed or mortgage is to be assumed, purchaser agrees to
apply for a loan assumption if required and agrees to pay (1) a loan transfer fee
not to exceed _____ Dollars ($_____) and (2) an interest
rate not to exceed _____ per cent (_____%) per annum. If the
loan to be assumed has provisions for a shared equity or variable interest rates
or variable payments, this contract is conditioned upon the purchaser reviewing
and consenting to such provisions. If the lender's consent to a loan assumption
is required, this contract is conditioned upon obtaining such consent without
change in the terms and conditions of such loan except as herein provided.

5. If a note is to be made payable to seller as partial or full payment of the
purchase price, this contract shall not be assignable by purchaser without written
consent of seller.

Page 4 of 13

CONTRACT FOR RESIDENTIAL CONDOMINIUM - Continued

6. Cost of any appraisal for loan purposes to be obtained after this date shall
be paid by _____ .
        (purchaser or as case may be)

7. An abstract of title to the property, certified to date, or a current
commitment for title insurance policy in an amount equal to the purchase price,
at seller's option and expense, shall be furnished to purchaser on or before

_____, 19____ . If seller elects to furnish said title insurance
(month and day)   (yr)

commitment, seller will deliver the title insurance policy to purchaser after
closing and pay the premium thereon.

8. The date of closing shall be the date for delivery of deed as provided in
SECTION TWO, Paragraph 1. The hour and place of closing shall be as designated by
mutual consent.

SECTION TWO - TITLE-

1. Title shall be merchantable in seller, except as stated in this Paragraph and
Paragraph 2. Subject to payment or tender as above provided and compliance by
purchaser with the other terms and provisions hereof, seller shall execute and
deliver a good and sufficient _____ warranty deed to
                                      (type of deed)

purchaser on _____, 19____, or, by mutual agreement, at an
                  (month and day)   (yr)

earlier date, conveying the property free and clear of all taxes, except the
general taxes for the year of closing, and except _____
                                                        (list any other taxes

_____
such as personal property taxes on income property, association dues , water fees

_____ ,
or dues, or insert "none")

CONTRACT FOR RESIDENTIAL CONDOMINIUM - Continued

free and clear of all liens for special improvements installed as of the date of purchaser's signature hereon, whether assessed or not; free and clear of all liens and encumbrances except _____

(list any loans remaining after closing which are to be

_____

assumed by purhcaser or wrapped, or insert "none")

_____,

and except recorded and/or apparent easements for telephone, electricity, water, sanitary sewer and easements for _____

(list easements or insert "none other")

_____

_____;

subject to the benefits and burdens of any Declaration of Covenants (hereinafter called Declaration) Articles of Incorporation of the Owners' Association (hereinafter Articles), Bylaws of the Owners' Association (hereinafter Bylaws) and party wall agreements; except the following restrictive covenants which do not contain a forfeiture or reverter clause: _____

(list any covenant or deed restriction

_____,

 or insert "none")

and subject to building and zoning regulations.

2. Except as stated in Paragraph 1 of this Section, if title is not merchantable and written notice of defect(s) is given by purchaser to seller on or before date of closing, seller shall use reasonable effort to correct such defect(s) prior to date of closing. If seller is unable to correct said defect(s) on or before date of closing, at seller's option and upon written notice to purchaser on or before date of closing, the date of closing shall be extended _____

(number)

days for the purpose of correcting said defect(s). If title is not rendered

CONTRACT FOR RESIDENTIAL CONDOMINIUM - Continued

merchantable as provided in this Paragraph 2, at purchaser's option, this contract shall be void and of no effect and each party hereto shall be released from all obligations hereunder and all payments and things of value received hereunder shall be returned to purchaser.

3. If the total indebtedness secured by liens on the property exceeds the purchase price, this contract shall be void and of no effect and each party hereto shall be released from all obligations hereunder and all payments and things of value received hereunder shall be returned to purchaser.

SECTION THREE - TAXES- General taxes for the year of closing, based on the most recent levy and the most recent assessment, prepaid rents, water rents, sewer rents, FHA mortgage insurance premiums and interest on encumbrances, and current regular Condominium or Owners' Association assessments, if any, and:

_____

(list other items remaining on property which will be pro-rated between purchaser

_____

and seller at closing; or insert "none")

_____

shall be apportioned to date of delivery of deed. Regular Condominium or Owners' Association assessments paid in advance shall be credited to seller at the time of closing. Cash reserves held out of the regular Condominium or Owners' Association for deferred maintenance by the Condominium or Owners' Association (hereinafter Owners' Association) shall not be credited to seller except as may be otherwise provided by the Declaration, Articles, or Bylaws. Any special assessment by the Owners' Association for improvements that have been installed as of the date of the purchaser's signature hereon shall be the obligation of the seller. Any other

Page 7 of 13

CONTRACT FOR RESIDENTIAL CONDOMINIUM - Continued

special assessment assessed prior to the date of closing by the Owners' Association shall be the obligation of _____.
                                                                    (purchaser/seller)

SECTION FOUR - POSSESSION OF PROPERTY AND RESPONSIBILITIES- Cross out Paragraph 1 or Paragraph 2:

    1.   Possession of the property shall be delivered to purchaser on date of delivery of deed;

OR

    2.   Possession of property shall be to plurchaser on or before the date of delivery of deed subject to a _____ term lease
                                                (amount of time)
or rental agreement with _____ as
                                    (name(s) of tenant(s))
tenant(s), which shall be assigned to purchaser at closing and which expires on _____, 19____.
                              (month and day)   (yr)

3. If seller fails to deliver possession on the date herein specified, seller shall be subject to eviction and shall be liable for a daily rental of _____ Dollars ($_____) until possession is delivered.

SECTION FIVE - DESTRUCTION OF PREMISES- In the event that the property is damaged by fire or other casualty prior to the time of closing in an amount of not more than ten percent of the total purchase price, seller shall be obligated to repair the same before the date herein provided for delivery of deed. In the event such damage cannot be repaired within said time or if damage shall exceed such sum, this contract may be terminated at the option of the purchaser and all payments

Page 8 of 13

CONTRACT FOR RESIDENTIAL CONDOMINIUM - Continued

and things of value received hereunder shall be returned to purchser. Should the purchaser elect to carry out this agreement despite such damage, purchaser shall be entitled to all the credit for the insurance proceeds resulting from such damage not exceeding, however, the total purchase price. Should any fixtures or services fail between the date of this agreement and the date of possession or the date of delivery of deed, whichever shall be earlier, then the seller shall be liable for the repair or replacement of such fixtures or services with a unit of similar size, age and quality, or an equivalent credit, but only to the extent that the maintenance or replacement of such fixtures or services is not the responsibility of the Owners' Association.

SECTION SIX - TIME OF ESSENCE; DEFAULT- Time is of the essence hereof. If any note or check received as earnest money hereunder or any other payment due hereunder is not paid, honored or tendered when due, or if any other obligation hereunder is not performed as herein provided, there shall be the following remedies:

1. **IF SELLER IS IN DEFAULT,** (a) purchaser may elect to treat this contract as terminated, in which case all payments and things of value received hereunder shall be returned to purchaser and purchaser may recover such damages as may be proper, or (b) purchaser may elect to treat this contract as being in full force and effect and purchaser shall have the right to an action for specific performance or damages or both.

2. **IF PURCHASER IS IN DEFAULT,** then all payments and things of value received hereunder shall be forfeited by purchaser and retained on behalf of seller and both parties shall thereafter be released from all obligations hereunder. It is agreed that such payments and things of value are **liquidated**

CONTRACT FOR RESIDENTIAL CONDOMINIUM - Continued

damages and (except as provided in Paragraph 3 of this Section) are the **seller's sole and only remedy** for the purchaser's failure to perform the obligations of this contract. Seller expressly waives the remedies of specific performance and additional damages.

SECTION SEVEN - ATTORNEYS' FEES- Anything to the contrary herein notwithstanding, in the event of any litigation arising out of this contract, the court may award to the prevailing party all reasonable costs and expenses, including attorneys' fees.

SECTION EIGHT - INCORPORATION OF CONDOMINIUM DOCUMENTS- Within _____
                                                                              (number)
calendar days of the date this instrument becomes a contract between the parties, seller agrees to deliver to purchaser a current copy of the Declaration, Articles, Bylaws and rules and regulations, if any. If purchaser shall give written notice of disapproval of any of these documents to seller within _____
                                                                                     (number)
calendar days (not less than 5) after receipt of such documents, this contract shall be terminated and all payments and things of value received hereunder shall be returned to purchaser. If no such timely written notice of disapproval is given, purchaser shall be deemed to have accepted and approved the terms of said documents, and purchaser's right to terminate this contract pursuant to this SECTION EIGHT shall be waived.

SECTION NINE - ASSESSMENTS- Seller represents that the amount of the regular Owners' Association assessment is currently _____ Dollars ($_____) per _____, and that there are no unpaid regular assessments against
     (week/month/year)
the property excepting the current regular assessment and except _____
                                                                        (list any
_____.
such exceptions or insert "none")

CONTRACT FOR RESIDENTIAL CONDOMINIUM - Continued

Such assessments are subject to change as provided in the Declaration, Articles, or Bylaws. Seller agrees to request, promptly and diligently, a statement of assessments against the property, prepared and certified by the Board of Directors of the Owners' Association or its designated agent, and deliver said statement to purchaser on or before time of closing unless not obtainable after due diligence. Any fees incident to the issuance of such statement of assessment shall be paid by seller.

SECTION TEN - APPROVAL- If the Declaration, Articles, or Bylaws require written approval of the sale contemplated by this contract or waiver of right of first refusal, seller shall, within _____ calendar days of the date this
(number)

instrument becomes a contract, request such approval and/or waiver as may be required and deliver it to purchaser on or before the time of closing. If seller shall be unable to obtain such approval and/or waiver on or before

_____, 19___, this contract shall be terminated and all payments
(month and day)   (yr)

and things of value received hereunder shall be returned to purchaser. Purchaser agrees to cooperate with seller in obtaining the approval and/or waiver and shall make available such information as the Owners' Association may reasonably require.

SECTION ELEVEN - ADDITIONAL PROVISIONS- _____
                                               (insert any added provisions or

_____
contingencies not included above)

_____

_____

_____

_____

Page 11 of 13

CONTRACT FOR RESIDENTIAL CONDOMINIUM - Continued

_____

_____ .

_____

_____

_____

SECTION TWELVE - CAPTIONS- The captions used herein are merely for easy reference and shall have no effect on the agreement or the terms and conditions herein contained.

SECTION THIRTEEN - BINDING EFFECT OF CONTRACT- If this proposal is accepted by seller in writing and purchaser receives notice of such acceptance on or before _____ o'clock _____.m., _____, 19____, this
                                                              (month and day)   (yr)
instrument shall become a contract between seller and purchaser and shall inure to the benefit of the heirs, successors and assigns of such parties, except as stated in SECTION ONE, Paragraph 5.

_____   _____
(Purchaser's signature)   (Date)   (Purchaser's signature)   (Date)

_____   _____
(Address)   (Address)

_____   _____
(City)   (City)

_____   _____
(County)   (County)

_____ .   _____ .
(State)   (State)

CONTRACT FOR RESIDENTIAL CONDOMINIUM - Continued

Seller accepts the above proposal this _____ day of

(number)

_____ , 19____ .

(month)   (yr)

_____   _____   _____   _____
(Seller's signature)   (Date)   (Seller's signature)   (Date)

_____   _____
(Address)   (Address)

_____   _____
(City)   (City)

_____   _____
(County)   (County)

_____ .   _____ .
(State)   (State)

CONTRACT TO BUY AND SELL REAL ESTATE: VACANT LAND

Agreement made _____, 19____, between:
　　　　　　　　　(month and day)　　　　　　　　(yr)

_____　and　_____
(Name(s) of seller)　　　　　　　　　　(Name(s) of purchaser)

herein referred to as seller, of　　　herein referred to as purchaser, of

_____　　　　　_____
(Address)　　　　　　　　　　　　　　(Address)

_____　　　　　_____
(City)　　　　　　　　　　　　　　　　(City)

_____　　　　　_____
(County)　　　　　　　　　　　　　　　(County)

_____　　　　　_____
(State)　　　　　　　　　　　　　　　　(State)

RECITALS

1.　The undersigned seller hereby acknowledges having received from

_____
(name(s) of person(s) or entity providing earnest money)

the sum of _____ Dollars ($_____) in the form of
　　　　　　　(amount of earnest money)

_____ to be held in a
(personal check/cashier's check/promissory note)

trust account at _____ Bank as earnest money and part
　　　　　　　　　(name of bank)

payment for the following described real estate in

_____
(Town/township/city/or as case may be)

_____
(County)

_____
(State)

Page 1 of 9

CONTRACT FOR REAL ESTATE: VACANT LAND - Continued

which is more particularly described as follows: _____
                                                        (legal description)

_____,

together with all easements and rights of way appurtenant thereto, and all

improvements thereon and all fixtures of a permanent nature currently on the

premises except as hereinafter provided, in their present condition, ordinary wear

and tear excepted, known as

_____
(Address)

_____
(City)

_____
(County)

_____
(State)

and hereinafter called the property.

2. The undersigned purchaser, _____,
                                   (name of purchaser(s) as they wish to take title)

as _____ hereby agree to buy the property and the
       (joint tenants/tenants in common)

seller hereby agrees to sell the property upon the terms and conditions stated

herein:

SECTION ONE - PURCHASE PRICE AND TERMS OF PAYMENT-   The purchase price shall be

1. U.S. _____ Dollars ($_____), payable as
         (full amount of purchase price)

follows: _____ Dollars ($_____) hereby
              (amount of earnest money)

receipted for; the balance of the purchase price shall be payable in the following

manner in U.S. currency, certified or cashier's funds: _____
                                                          (describe method of payment)

Page 2 of 9

CONTRACT FOR REAL ESTATE: VACANT LAND - Continued

_____

_____

_____

_____ .

2. Price to include _____
                          (list all inclusions)

_____

_____

_____ ,

and the following water rights: _____

_____

_____ .

3. If a new loan is to be obtained by purchaser from a third party, purchaser agrees to promptly and diligently (a) apply for such loan, (b) execute all documents and furnish all information and documents required by the lender, and (c) pay the customary costs of obtaining such loan. Then if such loan is not approved on or before _____, 19____, or if so approved but is not
                                   (month and day)   (yr)
available at time of closing, this contract shall be null and void and all payments and things of value received hereunder shall be returned to purchaser.

4. If a note and trust deed or mortgage is to be assumed, purchaser agrees to apply for a loan assumption if required and agrees to pay (1) a loan transfer fee not to exceed _____ Dollars ($_____) and (2) an interest rate not to exceed _____ per cent (_____%) per annum. If the loan to be assumed has provisions for a shared equity or variable interest rates

Page 3 of 9

CONTRACT FOR REAL ESTATE: VACANT LAND - Continued

or variable payments, this contract is conditioned upon the purchaser reviewing and consenting to such provisions. If the lender's consent to a loan assumption is required, this contract is conditioned upon obtaining such consent without change in the terms and conditions of such loan except as herein provided.

5. If a note is to be made payable to seller as partial or full payment of the purchase price, this contract shall not be assignable by purchaser without written consent of seller.

6. Cost of any appraisal for loan purposes to be obtained after this date shall be paid by _____.
       (purchaser or as case may be)

7. An abstract of title to the property, certified to date, or a current commitment for title insurance policy in an amount equal to the purchase price, at seller's option and expense, shall be furnished to purchaser on or before
_____, 19____. If seller elects to furnish said title insurance
(month and day)   (yr)
commitment, seller will deliver the title insurance policy to purchaser after closing and pay the premium thereon.

8. The date of closing shall be the date for delivery of deed as provided in SECTION TWO, Paragraph 1. The hour and place of closing shall be as designated by mutual consent.

SECTION TWO - TITLE-

1. Title shall be merchantable in seller, except as stated in this paragraph and in paragraphs 2 and 3 below, subject to payment or tender as above provided and compliance by purchaser with the other terms and provisions hereof. Seller shall

Page 4 of 9

CONTRACT FOR REAL ESTATE: VACANT LAND - Continued

execute and deliver a good and sufficient _____

                                              (type of deed)

warranty deed to purchaser on _____ , 19____ , or, by mutual

                              (month and day)   (yr)

agreement, at an earlier date, conveying the property free and clear of all taxes,

except the general taxes for the year of closing, and except _____

                                                            (list any other taxes

_____ ; and free and clear of all liens for

(or insert "none other")

special improvements installed as of the date of purchaser's signature hereon,

whether assessed or not; free and clear of all liens and encumbrances except

_____

(list any loans remaining after closing which purchaser is to assume,

_____

or insert "none")

_____ ,

and except the following specific recorded and/or apparent easements: _____

                                                                    (list any

_____

easements, or insert "none")

and subject to building and zoning regulations.

2. Except as stated in Paragraph 1 of this Section, if title is not merchantable

and written notice of defect(s) is given by purchaser to seller on or before date

of closing, seller shall use reasonable effort to correct such defect(s) prior to

date of closing. If seller is unable to correct said defect(s) on or before date

of closing, at seller's option and upon written notice to purchaser on or before

date of closing, the date of closing shall be extended _____

                                                        (number)

days for the purpose of correcting said defect(s). If title is not rendered

merchantable as provided in this paragraph, at purchaser's option, this contract

CONTRACT FOR REAL ESTATE: VACANT LAND - Continued

shall be void and of no effect and each party hereto shall be released from all obligations hereunder and all payments and things of value received hereunder shall be returned to purchaser.

3. If the total indebtedness secured by liens on the property exceeds the purchase price, this contract shall be void and of no effect and each party hereto shall be released from all obligations hereunder and all payments and things of value received hereunder shall be returned to purchaser.

SECTION THREE - TAXES- General taxes for the year of closing, based on the most recent levy and the most recent assessment, prepaid rents, water rents, sewer rents, FHA mortgage insurance premiums and interest on encumbrances, if any and

_____

(list other items remaining on property which will be pro-rated between purchaser

_____

and seller at closing; or insert "none")

_____

shall be apportioned to date of delivery of deed.

SECTION FOUR - POSSESSION OF PROPERTY AND RESPONSIBILITIES- Possession of the property shall be delivered to purchaser on the date of delivery of deed, subject to the following leases or tenancies: _____

_____

_____

_____.

SECTION FIVE - DESTRUCTION OF PROPERTY- In the event that the property is substantially damaged by fire or other casualty between the date of this contract

CONTRACT FOR REAL ESTATE: VACANT LAND - Continued

and the date of delivery of deed, purchaser may elect to terminate this contract; in which case all payments and things of value received hereunder shall be returned to purchaser.

SECTION SIX - TIME OF ESSENCE; DEFAULT- Time is of the essence hereof. If any note or check received as earnest money hereunder or any other payment due hereunder is not paid, honored or tendered when due, or if any other obligation hereunder is not performed as herein provided, there shall be the following remedies:

    1. **IF SELLER IS IN DEFAULT,** (a) purchaser may elect to treat this contract as terminated, in which case all payments and things of value received hereunder shall be returned to purchaser and purchaser may recover such damages as may be proper, or (b) purchaser may elect to treat this contract as being in full force and effect and purchaser shall have the right to an action for specific performance or damages or both.

    2. **IF PURCHASER IS IN DEFAULT,** then all payments and things of value received hereunder shall be forfeited by purchaser and retained on behalf of seller and both parties shall thereafter be released from all obligations hereunder. It is agreed that such payments and things of value are **liquidated damages** and (except as provided in Paragraph 3 of this Section) are the **seller's sole and only remedy** for the purchaser's failure to perform the obligations of this contract. Seller expressly waives the remedies of specific performance and additional damages.

CONTRACT FOR REAL ESTATE: VACANT LAND - Continued

SECTION SEVEN - ADDITIONAL PROVISIONS- _____
(insert any added provisions or

_____
contingencies not included above or insert "none other")

_____

_____

_____

_____

_____

_____

_____

SECTION EIGHT - CAPTIONS- The captions used herein are merely for easy reference and shall have no effect on the agreement or the terms and conditions herein contained.

SECTION NINE - BINDING EFFECT OF CONTRACT- If this proposal is accepted by seller in writing and purchaser receives notice of such acceptance on or before

_____ o'clock _____.m., _____, 19___, this
(month and day)   (yr)

instrument shall become a contract between seller and purchaser and shall inure to the benefit of the heirs, successors and assigns of such parties, except as stated in SECTION ONE, Paragraph 6.

CONTRACT FOR REAL ESTATE: VACANT LAND - Continued

_____
(Purchaser's signature)   (Date)

_____
(Address)

_____
(City)

_____
(County)

_____ .
(State)

_____
(Purchaser's signature)   (Date)

_____
(Address)

_____
(City)

_____
(County)

_____ .
(State)

THE FOLLOWING SECTION IS TO BE COMPLETED BY SELLER:

_____
(Seller's signature)   (Date)

_____
(Address)

_____
(City)

_____
(County)

_____ .
(State)

_____
(Seller's signature)   (Date)

_____
(Address)

_____
(City)

_____
(County)

_____ .
(State)

TENANTS IN COMMON: EQUITY-SHARING AGREEMENT

Agreement made _____, 19 ____, between:
         (month and day)   (yr)

_____	_____
(Name(s) of investor)	(Name(s) of co-investor)
herein known as investor, of	herein known as co-investor, of
_____	_____
(Address)	(Address)
_____	_____
(City)	(City)
_____	_____
(County)	(County)
_____	_____
(State)	(State)

RECITALS

Investor and co-investor desire to purchase that certain real property commonly known as:

_____
(Address)

_____
(City)

_____
(County)

_____
(State)

Therefore, it is mutually covenanted and agreed between the parties hereto, in consideration of the mutual promises and undertakings set forth herein, as follows:

SECTION ONE - TERM OF AGREEMENT- The term of this agreement shall be for a period of _____ months, unless otherwise agreed upon.
    (number)

Page 1 of 8

TENANTS IN COMMON: EQUITY-SHARING - Continued

SECTION TWO - VALUE OF PROPERTY- The value of said property is agreed to be the

purchase price of _____ Dollars ($_____).

SECTION THREE - INVESTOR'S INVESTMENT- The investor's investment on such property

shall be taken in investor's name, subject to required financing and security

documents. Investor shall convey to co-investor an undivided _____

percent (_____%) interest in such property conditioned upon full compliance by

co-investor with all of the terms of this agreement. Investor's investment is

_____ Dollars ($_____).

_____ Dollars ($_____) is being used to cover

the _____ Dollars ($_____) down payment
    (amount of down payment)

and _____ Dollars ($_____) to cover
    (amount of closing costs)

closing costs. The co-investor is making no initial investment in the property.

SECTION FOUR - TITLE- Title to said real property shall be taken as tenants in

common with investor having an undivided _____ percent (_____%)

interest therein.

SECTION FIVE - CONSIDERATION OF AND CONDITIONS OF INVESTOR'S INVESTMENT-

A. Each party acknowledges that the _____ percent (_____%) interest

in the property is subject to a deed of trust securing a promissory note given for

the balance of the purchase price in the amount of _____

_____ Dollars ($_____).

B. Co-investor shall pay on or before the due date each and every installment of

principal and interest (plus taxes and insurance if taxes and insurance are

TENANTS IN COMMON: EQUITY-SHARING - Continued

escrowed by the lender) to repay the loan described in Paragraph A of this Section

and in addition shall pay before the delinquency date each and every tax,

assessment, or other public charge levied upon or assessed against said property.

Each party shall be entitled to deduct _____ percent (_____%) of the

payment for interest, taxes and insurance in reporting taxable income to the

United States and to any state thereof.

C. Co-investor shall have the sole right to make any capital improvements to said

property without having first obtained the written consent of investor.

D. Co-investor shall not cause, suffer or permit any encumbrance to be placed on

said property during the continuance of this tenancy and hereby agrees to hold

investor harmless from any loss, costs, expense or damage suffered or incurred in

removing any encumbrances placed on said property in violation of the provisions

of this paragraph.

E. To the extent that the total depreciation on said property may be deductible

from the adjusted gross income of a person or persons who are legally entitled to

such depreciation, in reporting such person's taxable income to the United States

and to any state thereof, it is agreed between all parties that investor shall be

entitled to _____ percent (_____%) of such depreciation and that co-

investor shall not be entitled to claim any depreciation.   Co-investor agrees to

furnish investor with all necessary records for such purpose within _____

                                                                      (number)

days after each calendar year end for the term of this agreement.

F. Co-investor shall bear and pay any and all improvements or other assessments

that may be levied against said property.   Co-investor may contest any such

assessments, but not in any manner which will cause additional taxes, interest, or

penalties to be assessed against said property, nor in any manner which may cause

said property to be seized and sold or sold to effectuate payment of such

assessments.   If any such assessment levied against said property results in a

TENANTS IN COMMON: EQUITY-SHARING - Continued

permanent improvement thereto, such assessment shall be deemed to be the actual cost of improvements within the meaning of Paragraph E of this Section.

G. Co-investor agrees to maintain said property at co-investor's sole expense.

H. Co-investor shall not dispose of any real or personal property which is a part of said real property without written consent of investor.

I. Co-investor shall obtain and keep in force a policy or policies of fire insurance with extended coverage with limits of not less than the amount required to replace the improvements on subject property and public liability insurance limits of not less than _____ Dollars ($_____) naming the parties hereto as insureds, insuring said property against the usual perils covered by said policies. Co-investor shall bear and pay all premiums for such insurance. In the event of a total loss, co-investor shall assign co-investor's interest in any insurance claim to the investor to cover investor's investment, including any costs of settling the insurance claim. Any excess monies will be divided equally between the investor and co-investor.

SECTION SIX - ENCUMBRANCES AND ASSIGNMENTS- Co-investor shall not sell, transfer, assign or encumber co-investor's interests in the property, this agreement, or lease of the property without the prior written consent of the investor.

SECTION SEVEN - DEFAULT BY CO-INVESTOR- The occurrence of any of the following shall constitute a default by co-investor:

A. Failure to make any payment required herein, if the failure continues for _____ days after notice has been given to the co-investor.
(number)

B. Abandonment and vacation of the premises (failure to occupy the premises) for _____ consecutive days shall be deemed abandonment and vacation,
(number)

unless notice to investor is given in advance and investor consents thereto.

Page 4 of 8

C. Failure to perform any other provision of this agreement, if the failure to perform is not cured within _____ days after notice has been given to
(number)
investor.

Notices given under this paragraph shall specify the alleged default and the applicable agreement provisions, and shall demand the co-investor perform the provisions of this agreement or make the lease or purchase payment that is in arrears, as the case may be, within the applicable period of time, or quit the premises. No such notice shall be deemed a forfeiture or a termination of this agreement unless investor so elects in the notice.

SECTION EIGHT - INVESTOR'S REMEDIES IN CASE OF DEFAULT- Investor shall have the following remedies if co-investor commits default. These remedies are not exclusive; they are cumulative in addition to any remedies now or later allowed by law.

A. If co-investor commits any default under SECTION SEVEN herein, investor may take possession of the premises in the manner provided by the laws of unlawful detainer in the State of _____ in effect at the date of such default. Co-investor agrees that co-investor's right to possession of the premises shall terminate by such default, notwithstanding ownership of an undivided _____ percent (_____%) interest in the premises.

B. Co-investor acknowledges that if any monthly payment owed is not made when due, investor will incur costs, the exact amount of which is extremely difficult and impractical to fix. Therefore, co-investor shall pay to investor an additional sum of _____ percent (_____%) of the overdue payment as a late charge. The parties agree that this late charge represents a fair and reasonable estimate of the costs that investor will incur by reason of any late payment by co-investor. Acceptance of any late charge shall not constitute a

TENANTS IN COMMON: EQUITY-SHARING - Continued

waiver of co-investor's default with respect to the overdue amount, or prevent investor from exercising any of the other rights and remedies available to them.

C. Upon the signing of this agreement, a request for notice of default shall be given to all lenders on behalf of the investor. If co-investor fails to make payment when due, investor may cure the default at co-investor's cost. Any sums paid by the investor shall be due immediately from the co-investor, and if not paid shall bear interest at the rate of _____ percent (_____%) per annum until paid.

If co-investor does not cure their default within _____ days after
(number)

notice has been given by investor, the investor may thereafter, at investor's option, make all payments directly to the holder of the note and of the policies of insurance covering the premises and to the appropriate governmental authority for tax and assessment payments due on such property.

SECTION NINE - OPTIONS TO PURCHASE OR SELL- Each party shall have the right to purchase the interest of the other party in such premises on the following terms and conditions:

A. At any time during the term hereof, co-investor may purchase investor's interest in the subject property for an amount equal to investor's investment plus _____ percent (_____%) of net appreciation. Net appreciation" shall be defined as: appraised value at time of buy-out, less present value (per SECTION TWO) less transfer costs. During the first _____ months, the net
(number)

appreciation shall be computed either by increasing present value _____ percent (_____%) per month, or by using appraised value, whichever is greater.

B. If co-investor should elect not to purchase investor's interest as set forth above, investor shall have the option to purchase co-investor's interest for

Page 6 of 8

_____ of net appreciation, minus the investor's investment.
(amount)

C. By mutual agreement, investor and co-investor may extend this contract for an additional period of time.

D. Should investor and co-investor elect none of the above, it is agreed by both parties that the property shall be sold at the appraised value or price mutually agreed upon. Upon the sale of the property, the net proceeds shall be distributed as follows:

   (1) Investor first shall receive a sum equal to investor's investment, and reimbursement for any other payments made by investor on the property.

   (2) The remainder of the sale price shall be divided equally between investor and co-investor after all costs of sale have been deducted.

SECTION TEN - CO-OPERATION ON EXCHANGE- If requested by investor, co-investor agrees to co-operate with investor to effect a tax-deferred exchange under Section 1031 of the Internal Revenue Code and further agrees to execute any and all documents necessary for said tax-deferred exchange. Said co-operation shall be at no cost or liability to co-investor.

SECTION ELEVEN - NOTICES- Any and all notices and other communications required or permitted by this agreement shall be served on or given to either party by the other party in writing and shall be deemed duly served and given when personally delivered to any of the parties to whom it is directed, or in lieu of such personal service, when deposited in the United States mail, first class postage prepaid, addressed to investor at

TENANTS IN COMMON: EQUITY-SHARING - Continued

_____
(Address)

_____
(City)

_____
(State)

or co-investor at the property address or such forwarding address that the co-investor has given to the investor.

SECTION TWELVE - ATTORNEYS' FEES- In the event any legal action is brought by either party to enforce the terms hereof or relating to the demised premises, the prevailing party shall be entitled to all costs incurred in connection with such action, including reasonable attorneys' fees as determined by the Court.

This agreement is binding upon the parties hereto, their heirs, successor and assigns.

_____
(Signature of investor)

_____
(Signature of investor)

_____
(Signature of co-investor)

_____
(Signature of co-investor)

III. CONTRACTUAL CLAUSES

ADDENDUM

RE: Contract dated _____ , 19____ , between:
          (month and day)   (yr)

_____ and   _____
(Name(s) of purchaser)   (Name(s) of seller)

herein known as purchaser, of   herein known as seller, of

_____   _____
(Address)   (Address)

_____   _____
(City)   (City)

_____   _____
(County)   (County)

_____   _____
(State)   (State)

relating to sale and purchase of property known as _____
                                           (legal description of property)

_____

_____

also known as   _____
                   (Address)

                  _____
                   (City)

                  _____
                   (County)

                  _____
                   (State)

ADDENDUM - Continued

The changes in said contract are _____

(list changes in contract)

_____

_____

_____

_____

_____

_____

_____

_____

_____

_____

_____

_____

Dated this _____ day of _____, 19____ .

(number)   (month)   (yr)

_____   _____

(Purchaser's signature)   (Seller's signature)

_____   _____

(Purchaser's signature)   (Seller's signature)

ADDENDUM: OWNER CARRY-BACK-FINANCING PROVISION

Financing provision addendum made _____, 19____, between:
                                   (month and day)   (yr)

                    and

_____   _____
(Name(s) of seller)   (Name(s) of purchaser)

herein referred to as seller, of   herein referred to as purchaser, of

_____   _____
(Address)   (Address)

_____   _____
(City)   (City)

_____   _____
(County)   (County)

_____   _____
(State)   (State)

1. THIS ADDENDUM is attached to and is part of the _____
                                           (specify contract)

_____

contract dated the _____ day of _____, 19____, between
                (number)   (month)   (yr)

_____ and _____
(name(s) of purchaser)   (name(s) of seller)

and relating to the following property _____
                                   (legal description of property)

_____,

also known as   _____
                    (Address)

                    _____
                    (City)

                    _____
                    (County)

                    _____.
                    (State)

ADDENDUM: FINANCING PROVISION - Continued

2. The promissory note which shall be signed by purchaser and accepted by seller shall be _____,
(specify state form used)

and shall be secured by a deed of trust for the benefit of seller. The deed of trust which shall be signed by purchaser and accepted by seller shall be

_____.
(identity of state form used)

Copies of these forms are attached to this contract and are incorporated herein by this reference.

The forms will be completed with appropriate terms in accordance with this contract, which terms will include, but not be limited to the following:

a) The interest rate to be charged on the unpaid principal balance will be

_____ per cent (_____%) per annum; seller agrees to carry financing:

b) Cross out either Alternative 1 or Alternative 2:

Alternative 1 - Payments will be due and payable on the

_____ day of each and every month after closing , and all
(number)

principal and accrued but unpaid interest will be due and payable in full

on _____, 19____;
(month and day)   (yr)

OR

Alternative 2 - The first payment will be due and payable

_____ days following the date of closing, and subsequent
(number)

payments will be due and payable on a like day of each month thereafter;

all principal and accrued but unpaid interest will be due and payable in

full on _____, 19____;
(month and day)   (yr)

Page 2 of 4

ADDENDUM: FINANCING PROVISION - Continued

c)   There shall be no restriction on prepayment in whole or in part except

_____ ;

(describe any prepayment penalty or insert "none")

d)   The purchaser shall pay a late charge equal to _____ per cent

(_____%) of any payment not received by the seller within _____

(number)

days of the due date of such payment;

e)   The interest rate upon default shall be _____ per cent (____%)

per annum;

f)   The interest rate applicable to sums advanced by the lender under Paragraph

_____ of the deed of trust shall be _____ per cent

(number)

(_____%) per annum;

g)   Paragraph _____ of the deed of trust _____ be

(number)   (will/will not)

deleted;

h)   Seller and purchaser agree that the printed portion of these forms will be

used as written and no deletions or changes shall be made thereto except as

follows: _____

(include provisions to be part of note and deed of trust not part

of standard contracts)

_____

_____

_____ .

3.   Purchaser agrees to provide seller with a complete and accurate financial

statement setting forth pertinent financial information relating to the purchaser,

ADDENDUM: FINANCING PROVISION - Continued

including but not being limited to employment, assets, liabilities, and net
worth, within _____ business days following acceptance of this
                    (number)

contract. Purchaser agrees that the seller shall be authorized to obtain a curent
credit report from a credit-reporting agency of seller's choice, following
execution of this contract. The obligations of the seller under this contract are
contingent upon the seller's review of that financial information, and approval of
the purchaser's credit worthiness, which approval shall not be reasonably
withheld. The seller shall notify the purchaser of any disapproval of the
purchaser within _____ business days after receipt by the seller of
                         (number)

this contract, or within _____ business days after receipt by the
                              (number)

seller of purchaser's financial statement, whichever shall occur later. In the
event written notice of disapproval is not received within the time period
designated, the seller shall be deemed to have approved the purchaser's
worthiness.

4. Both purchaser and seller understand it is advisable that each party seek
legal and tax advice relating to this transaction.

_____   _____
(Seller's signature)   (Purchaser's signature)

_____   _____
(Seller's signature)   (Purchaser's signature)

ADDENDUM TO CONTRACT FOR NEW HOME PURCHASE

RE: Contract dated _____, 19____, between:
(month and day)   (yr)

_____   and   _____
(Name(s) of purchaser)   (Name(s) of seller)

herein known as purchaser, of   herein known as seller, of

_____   _____
(Address)   (Address)

_____   _____
(City)   (City)

_____   _____
(County)   (County)

_____   _____
(State)   (State)

relating to the sale and purchase of property known as _____
                                                       (legal description of

_____
property)

_____

and also known as   _____
                         (Address)

                         _____
                         (City)

                         _____
                         (County)

                         _____
                         (State)

Page 1 of 2

ADDENDUM: NEW HOME PURCHASE - Continued

1. The seller warrants that a soil investigation has been or will be conducted by a registered engineer and a written report will be delivered to purchaser prior to date for delivery of deed, and that all foundations, footings and substructures will be constructed in accordance with the recommendations fo said engineer.

2. This construction will be completed according to terms set forth in the contract barring delays caused by strikes, acts of God, climate conditions, inability to obtain materials, acts of delay caused by purchaser and delays beyond the control of seller.

3. If due to circumstances beyond the control of seller, completion of construction is delayed, the seller is granted a reasonable extension of time to fulfill seller's obligation under this contract.

4. Seller guarantees to purchaser herein to correct any fault or defect in the property exclusively attributable to faulty workmanship or inferior materials in accordance with the Home Owner's Warranty Program, if one exists, or for a period of one year from the date of delivery of deed.

Dated this _____ day of _____, 19____ .
          (number)   (month)   (yr)

_____
(Signature of purchaser)

_____
(Signature of purchaser)

_____
(Signature of seller)

_____
(Signature of seller)

ADDENDUM: VA OR FHA FINANCING

This is a VA or FHA financing addendum to a contract made

_____, 19____, between:
(month and day)   (yr)

_____ and _____
(Name(s) of seller)   (Name(s) of purchaser)

herein referred to as seller, of   herein referred to as purchaser, of

_____   _____
(Address)   (Address)

_____   _____
(City)   (City)

_____   _____
(County)   (County)

_____   _____
(State)   (State)

concerning the following property _____
                                  (legal description of property)

_____,

and also known as   _____
                       (Address)

                      _____
                       (City)

                      _____
                       (County)

                      _____.
                       (State)

1. VETERANS ADMINISTRATION CONTRACT ADDENDUM (applicable/not applicable)

Initials _____ _____ _____ _____

It is expressly agreed that, notwithstanding any other provisions of this sales

agreement contract, the veteran/purchaser shall not incur any penalty by

ADDENDUM: VA OR FHA FINANCING - Continued

forfeiture of earnest money or otherwise be obligated to complete the purchase of the property described herein, if the contract purchase price or cost exceeds the reasonable value of the property established by the Veterans Administration. The veteran/purchaser shall, however, have the privilege and option of proceeding with the consumation of this contract without regard to the amount of the reasonable value established by the Veterans Administration.

2. **FHA CONTRACT AMMENDMENT** (applicable/not applicable)

      Initials _____ _____ _____ _____

It is expressly agreed that notwithstanding any other provisions of this contract, the purchaser shall not be obligated to complete the purchase of the property described herein or to incur any penalty by forfeiture of earnest money deposits or otherwise unless the seller has delivered to the purchaser a written statement issued by the Federal Housing Commissioner setting forth the appraised values of the property (excluding closing costs) of not less than _____ Dollars ($_____), which statement the seller hereby agrees to deliver to the purchaser promptly after such appraised value statement is made available to the seller. The purchaser shall, however, have the privilege and option of proceeding with the consumation of this contract without regard to the amount of the appraised valuation made by the Federal Housing Commissioner. **The appraised valuation is arrived at to determine the maximum mortgage the Department of Housing and Urban Development will insure. HUD does not warrant the value or the condition of the property. The purchaser should satisfy himself/herself/ themselves that the price and condition of the property are acceptable.**

ADDENDUM: VA OR FHA FINANCING - Continued

3. FHA SIDE AGREEMENT (applicable/not applicable)

Initials _____ _____ _____ _____

We, the undersigned, the seller and purchaser involved in this transaction, each certify that the terms of the contract for purchase are true to the best of our knowledge and belief, and that any other agreement entered into by any of these parties in connection with this transaction is attached to the sales agreement.

4. FHA-245 (applicable/not applicable)

Initials _____ _____ _____ _____

Purchaser certifies that purchaser fully understands the obligation undertaken, that purchaser's mortgage payment to principal and interest will start at

_____ Dollars ($_____) and will increase by

_____ per cent (_____%) each year for _____ years to
                                                        (number)

a maximum payment of _____ Dollars ($_____) and the

mortgage balance will increase to no more than _____ Dollars at

the end of the _____ year. The maximum total amount by which the
                  (number)

deferred interest shall increase the principal is _____ Dollare

($_____). Monthly installments shall be due according to the following

schedule:

Principal & Interest		Mortgage Insurance Premium	
$_____	during the 1st note year	$_____	during the 1st note year
$_____	during the 2nd note year	$_____	during the 2nd note year
$_____	during the 3rd note year	$_____	during the 3rd note year
$_____	during the 4th note year	$_____	during the 4th note year
$_____	during the 5th note year	$_____	during the 5th note year
$_____	during the 6th note year	$_____	during the 6th note year

Page 3 of 4

ADDENDUM: VA OR FHA FINANCING - Continued

$_____ during the 7th note year $_____ during the 7th note year

$_____ during the 8th note year $_____ during the 8th note year

$_____ during the 9th note year $_____ during the 9th note year

$_____ during the 10th note year $_____ during the 10th note yea

$_____ during the 11th note year $_____ during the 11th note yea

and thereafter   and will continue to

decline thereafter.

In addition, purchaser will be required to make payments toward taxes, hazard insurance and other costs of home ownership.

5. SELLER'S DISCOUNT FEE (applicable/not applicable)

Initials _____ _____ _____ _____

Seller agrees to pay a loan discount fee not to exceed _____ per cent (_____%) of said loan to the loan company making the loan to purchaser herein upon delivery of deed.

6. ADDITIONAL PROVISIONS: _____
(list any additional provisions)

_____

_____

_____

_____

_____

_____.

_____   _____
(Purchaser's signature)   (Seller's signature)

_____   _____
(Purchaser's signature)   (Seller's signature)

COUNTERPROPOSAL

RE: Proposed contract dated _____, 19____, between:
                          (month and day)   (yr)

_____   and   _____
(Name(s) of purchaser as their   (Name of seller as they hold title)
 names appear on sales contract)

herein known as purchaser, of   herein known as seller, of

_____   _____
(Address)   (Address)

_____   _____
(City)   (City)

_____   _____
(County)   (County)

_____   _____
(State)   (State)

said contract relating to the sale and purchase of property known as

_____
(legal description of property)

and also known as   _____
                          (Address)

                          _____
                          (City)

                          _____
                          (County)

                          _____
                          (State)

The undersigned seller accepts said proposed contract, subject to the following
ammendments: _____
             (list proposed changes in contract)

_____

_____

_____

_____

COUNTERPROPOSAL - Continued

_____

_____

_____

_____

_____

_____

_____

_____

_____

_____

All other terms and conditions shall remain the same. If this counterproposal is accepted by purchaser, as evidenced by purchaser's signature hereon, and if seller receives notice of such acceptance on or before _____, 19____,
  (month and day)   (yr)

the said proposed contract, as ammended hereby, shall become a contract between the parties.

_____   _____
(Signature of seller)   (Signature of seller)

The foregoing counterproposal is accepted this _____ day of
                                                        (number)
_____, 19____.
  (month)   (yr)

_____   _____
(Signature of purchaser)   (Signature of purchaser)

NOTE: When this counterproposal is ussed, the said proposed contract
         is NOT to be signed by seller. This counterproposal must be
         securely attached to said proposed contract.

DISCLAIMER CLAUSE: NEW CONSTRUCTION

RE: Property known as _____

                        (legal description of property)

_____

and also known as

                 _____
                 (Address)

                 _____
                 (City)

                 _____
                 (County)

                 _____
                 (State)

In connection with purchase of the above described property, the purchaser has been advised by _____ to make such investigations as
                   (seller/builder)
purchaser deems advisable to determine that the property, its component parts, appurtenances, fixtures, including the options and model of house, are in accordance with their agreement and understanding to be furnished by the

_____. Purchaser is advised to have soil tests made by a
(seller/builder)
qualified engineer to determine filled ground, underground water, bentonite (or any other chemical or mineral substances of any kind) which might prove deleterious or detrimental in the use of the land, verifying the zoning restrictions, lack of utilities (including gas, water, and sewer taps), the exact size of the residence or the size of the ground on which the house is to be constructed, or any other matters of any kind affecting the property.

Purchaser acknowledges purchaser has not and does not rely upon

_____ with reference to any matter relating to the said
(seller/builder)
property or its appurtenances and fixtures, including the completion date or quality of construction, excepting those which are specifically ennumerated in this contract.

Page 1 of 1

DISCLAIMER CLAUSE: USED HOME SALES

RE: Property known as _____

(legal description of property)

_____

and also known as   _____

(Address)

_____

(City)

_____

(County)

_____

(State)

    In connection with purchase of the above described property, the purchaser has been advised by _____ to make such investigations as

(seller/builder)
purchaser deems advisable to determine that the property, its component parts, appurtenances and fixtures are in accordance with their agreement and understanding to be furnished by the _____. Further, that

       (seller/builder)
the purchaser shall have inspections made by a qualified engineer to determine filled ground, underground water, bentonite (or any other chemical or mineral substances of any kind) which might prove deleterious or detrimental in the use of the land, verifying the zoning, restrictions, lack of utilities (including gas, water and sewer taps), or any other matters of any kind affecting the property.

    Further, that the purchaser has not and does not rely upon the

_____ with reference to any matter relating to the said

(seller/builder)
property or its appurtenances and fixtures, including the completion date or quality of construction.

FIRST RIGHT OF REFUSAL

RE: Contract dated _____, 19____, between:
                (month and day)   (yr)

_____ and _____
(Name(s) of purchaser)   (Name(s) of seller)

herein known as purchaser, of   herein known as seller, of

_____   _____
(Address)   (Address)

_____   _____
(City)   (City)

_____   _____
(County)   (County)

_____   _____
(State)   (State)

relating to the sale and purchase of property known as _____
                             (legal description of

_____
property)

and also known as   _____
                    (Address)

                    _____
                    (City)

                    _____
                    (County)

                    _____
                    (State)

    This contract is expressly conditional upon the sale and closing of the purchaser's property located at

Page 1 of 2

FIRST RIGHT OF REFUSAL - Continued

_____
(Address)

_____
(City)

_____
(County)

_____;
(State)

however, the seller hereto shall have the right to continue to offer the property herein described for sale. In the event another acceptable contract is received, the purchaser hereto shall be notified and given _____
(time in hours or days)
to remove said contingency set forth hereinabove and perform as agreed. Said notice may be personally delivered or mailed by certified mail to the purchaser named herein at the address set forth above. In the event of mailing, such notice shall be deemed to have been given on the date following the day of mailing, evidenced by the receipt of mailing held by seller. In the event the day following the date of the receipt of mailing is a non-mail day, notice shall be deemed to have been given at 12:01 A.M. of the next mail delivery day. If the purchaser hereto does not notify the seller in writing within

_____ that it is purchaser's intention to perform,
(time in hours or days)
the purchaser shall automatically release the seller from any further obligation to this contract and all deposits shall be returned forthwith to purchaser.

Dated this _____ day of _____, 19____.
         (number)   (month)   (yr)

_____   _____
(Purchaser's signature)   (Seller's signature)

_____   _____
(Purchaser's signature)   (Seller's signature)

Page 2 of 2

IV. CLOSING

AGREEMENT TO ENTER PROPERTY PRIOR TO CLOSING

Agreement made _____ , 19____ , between:
(month and day)   (yr)

_____ and _____
(Name(s) of seller)   (Name(s) of purchaser)

herein referred to as seller, of   herein referred to as purchaser, of

_____   _____
(Address)   (Address)

_____   _____
(City)   (City)

_____   _____
(County)   (County)

_____   _____
(State)   (State)

This agreement is made between purchaser and seller of the property known as:

_____
(legal description of property)

_____ ,

and also known as   _____
                            (Address)

                            _____
                            (City)

                            _____
                            (County)

                            _____ .
                            (State)

Purchaser agrees to accept property in "as is" condition.

Purchaser agrees to release seller of all liability against seller or workers on said property.

Page 1 of 2

AGREEMENT TO ENTER PRIOR TO CLOSING - Continued

Purchaser also agrees that seller will not be held responsible for payment of work completed on said property if sale is not consumated.

Should purchaser place personal possessions on premises, it is agreed and understood that seller is released of all liability from damage or destruction to said possessions. Purchaser shall provide evidence of homeowners insurance being in force.

This agreement is contingent upon purchaser having already obtained a firm mortgage commitment for above property as per sales contract between seller and purchaser dated _____, 19___. This agreement is intended
                      (month and day)   (yr)
solely for purchaser to enter premises prior to closing with seller's intent to grant possession.

Should purchaser not close, _____ Dollars ($_____) earnest money will be forfeited.

_____
(Seller's signature)   (Purchaser's signature)

_____
(Seller's signature)   (Purchaser's signature)

CLOSING INFORMATION FORM FOR TITLE COMPANY

_____
(Name of title company)

_____
(Address)

_____
(City)

_____
(County)

_____
(State)

Date _____ 19____   Closer's Name _____
    (month and day)   (yr)

Property address: _____
    (Address)

    _____
    (City)

    _____
    (County)

    _____
    (State)

Any new construction/improvements within the last six months? _____

    If so, please briefly describe: _____

_____

_____

Selling agent: _____   Phone: _____

Seller(s): _____   Attend closing? _____

CLOSING INFORMATION - Continued

Address after closing:

_____
(Address)

_____
(City)

_____
(County)

_____
(State)

Purchaser(s): _____ Attend closing? _____

Occupying property? _____

Taking occupancy as: _____ Joint tenants _____ Tenants in common

Earnest money: _____ Dollars ($_____)

_____ cash _____ check _____ note

To be redeemed: _____ Date _____

Financing: Purchase price: _____ Dollars ($_____)

New loan amount: _____ Dollars ($_____)

Name and address of lender:

_____
(Name)

_____
(Address)

_____
(City)

_____
(County)

_____
(State)

Phone _____

==============================

CLOSING INFORMATION - Continued

Assumption: _____

LOAN NUMBER **(IMPERATIVE!!)** _____

    Name and address of lender:

        _____
        (Name)

        _____
        (Address)

        _____
        (City)

        _____
        (County)

        _____
        (State)

        Phone _____

Other existing loans to be paid off: _____

    LOAN NUMBER(S): _____

    Name and address of lender:

        _____
        (Name)

        _____
        (Address)

        _____
        (City)

        _____
        (County)

        _____
        (State)

        Phone _____

Private party payoff(s): _____

    Name and address for payoff request:

CLOSING INFORMATION - Continued

_____
(Name)

_____
(Address)

_____
(City)

_____
(County)

_____
(State)

Phone _____

Rents: _____ Dollars ($_____) per month

Paid to:

_____
(Name)

_____
(Address)

_____
(City)

_____
(County)

_____
(State)

Phone _____

Water District: _____

Sewer District: _____

Special assessments: _____

Homeowners' Association: _____

Page 4 of 5

CLOSING INFORMATION - Continued

Contact for payment information:

(Name) _____

(Address) _____

(City) _____

(County) _____

(State) _____

Phone _____

Hazard insurance: _____ Agent phone: _____

Commission total: _____ Check to listing office? _____

Split? _____ Listing office: _____

Selling office: _____

Date of closing: _____, 19____
_____(month and day)_____ __(yr)__

Additional information (such as special circumstances, mail-outs, power of

attorney, forms used, etc.): _____

_____

_____

_____

_____

_____.

RENTAL BEFORE CLOSING AGREEMENT

Agreement made _____, 19____, between:
               (month and day)   (yr)

_____   and   _____
(Name(s) of seller)   (Name(s) of purchaser)

herein referred to as seller, of   herein referred to as purchaser, of

_____   _____
(Address)   (Address)

_____   _____
(City)   (City)

_____   _____
(County)   (County)

_____   _____
(State)   (State)

WHEREAS, the purchaser is purchasing from the seller a home located at

_____
(Address)

_____
(City)

_____
(County)

_____
(State)

and legally described as _____
                       (legal description of property)

_____;

NOW, THEREFORE, in consideration of the seller allowing the purchaser to take

possession prior to the final closing of the transaction under the purchase

contract dated _____, 19____, it is agreed as follows:
         (month and day)   (yr)

RENTAL BEFORE CLOSING AGREEMENT - Continued

SECTION ONE - The purchaser hereby accepts said home as having been delivered in accordance with all specifications and full compliance with all provisions of the above referred to purchase contract, and purchaser does hereby agree that the seller has performed all of the conditions and terms agreed thereof, and purchaser has removed all conditions in the purchase agreement, excepting that of obtaining

_____.

(a new loan, or as the case may be)

SECTION TWO - The purchaser shall be permitted to occupy the above described premises prior to delivery of the deed to the purchaser, and the payment of the balance of purchase price to seller. Nothing in this agreement shall convey any interest in and to the aforementioned property to the purchaser.

SECTION THREE - Exxcept as hereinafter set forth, purchaser agrees to pay to seller rental for the above described premises at the rate of _____ Dollars ($_____) per _____ from the date of occupancy,
                                          (week/month)
which shall be _____, 19____ and until the sale has been
               (month and day)   (yr)
completed, title has been transferred, and the seller has received full payment for the purchase price. Said rental amount shall be payable at closing.

SECTION FOUR - Purchaser agrees to arrange for transfer of all utilities into
_____ name as of date of occupancy, to pay all utility bills
(his/her/their)
incurred during the occupancy of the premises, and to pay all deposits for water, lights, gas or fuel oil, and other utilities as may be required.

Page 2 of 4

RENTAL BEFORE CLOSING AGREEMENT - Continued

SECTION FIVE - It is expressly understood and agreed that no part of any money classified and paid as rent shall be applied toward the purchase price of the above-described property, either in the form of down payment or mortgage closing costs.

SECTION SIX - Seller shall have the right to deduct any delinquent or past due rent or utility charges from moneys paid to seller under aforementioned purchase contract, and the purchaser does hereby authorize and direct seller to make said deductions from any such moneys.

SECTION SEVEN - Purchaser acknowledges that by accepting possession of the subject property prior to closing, the purchaser accepts said property, improvements, appurtenances and other items contained in contract thereon in their present condition, and that the said present condition is acceptable. Purchaser agrees to close the sale and transfer of the subject property as designated by seller, and that no objection will be made concerning the condition of the subject property by purchaser.

SECTION EIGHT - The seller agrees to maintain adequate insurance on the property, herein before described, until delivery of deed, and purchaser agrees to provide _____ insurance for _____ own personal property and carry
(his/her/their)   (his/her/their)
adequate liability insurance in favor of both seller and purchaser.

SECTION NINE - Earnest money deposit received by seller on the sales contract shall be applied as a damage deposit under this rental agreement, and shall be released to seller _____, 19____.
(month and day)   (yr)

Page 3 of 4

RENTAL BEFORE CLOSING AGREEMENT - Continued

SECTION TEN - In the event the purchaser fails to comply with the provisions of this rental agreement, the seller of the property shall be entitled to all costs and reasonable attorneys' fees enforcing the same.

Read and approved this _____ day of _____, 19____.
(number)   (month)   (yr)

_____   _____
(Seller's signature)   (Purchaser's signature)

_____   _____
(Seller's signature)   (Purchaser's signature)

V. RELEASES

RELEASE OF LIEN AGAINST REALTY

Dated _____, 19____
      (month and day)   (yr)

_____ and _____
(Name of judgment debtor)   (Name of judgment creditor)

herein referred to as judgment debtor   herein referred to as judgment creditor
of   of

_____   _____
(Address)   (Address)

_____   _____
(City)   (City)

_____   _____
(County)   (County)

_____   _____
(State)   (State)

In consideration of _____ Dollars ($_____),

paid to me by judgment debtor, receipt whereof is hereby acknowledged, I, judgment

creditor, do hereby release property in the

_____,
(County of)

_____.
(State of)

The property is more fully described as _____

_____,

The property is released from all claim to or interest in the same, or any part

thereof, which I may have under and by virtue of the judgment rendered on

_____, 19____,
(month and day)   (yr)

in _____
(name of court)

RELEASE OF LIEN AGAINST REALTY - Continued

against judgment debtor for the sum of _____
                                    (judgment to include costs, interest and

_____Dollars ($_____), and from all liens or encumbrances
attorney's fees)

that have attached to the same by reason of the recovery of the judgment as free

and clear, in all respects, as though the judgment had not been rendered.

_____
(Signature of judgment creditor)

ANTICIPATORY WAIVER OF LIEN

Waiver given _____, 19 _____ between:
                    (month and day)   (yr)

_____   _____
(Name of potential claimant)   (Name of owner)

herein known as potential claimant, of   herein known as owner, of

_____   _____
(Address)   (Address)

_____   _____
(City)   (City)

_____   _____
(County)   (County)

_____   _____
(State)   (State)

On _____, 19 _____, _____
        (month)   (yr)   (name of potential claimant)

entered into a contract with _____ to service
                              (name of owner)

the following property: _____
                         (designate and describe property)

_____

, of _____ by the following method _____
      (owner)   (describe labor

to be performed and/or materials to be furnished)_____

_____

_____.

   In consideration of _____ Dollars

($_____), receipt of which is acknowledged or as part of the

consideration of receiving the above-described contract, _____
                                                          (potential claimant)

Page 1 of 2

ANTICIPATORY WAIVER OF LIEN - Continued

waives all claims of lien and right of lien that he may obtain against such property by performing the above-described services.

In witness whereof, _____ has executed this
                  (potential claimant)

waiver in the City of _____, State of

_____ the day and year first above written.

_____   _____
(Signature of potential claimant)   (Signature of owner)

WAIVER OF EXISTING LIEN

The undersigned,

_____
(Name)

_____
(Address)

_____
(City)

_____
(County)

_____
(State)

has full knowledge of his right to a lien on the following property: _____
(designate

_____
and describe property)

_____

_____

of

_____
(Name of owner)

_____
(Address)

_____
(City)

_____
(County)

_____
(State)

for _____
(describe labor performed and/or materials furnished)

_____

_____

WAIVER OF EXISTING LIEN - Continued

pursuant to,_____
                   (cite statute or designate by what authority right to lien exists)

_____.

The undersigned, for the valuable consideration of _____

Dollars ($_____), receipt of which is acknowledged, voluntarily waives

all claims of lien and right of lien on the above-described property.

   In witness whereof, the undersigned has executed this waiver in the City of

_____, State of _____, on

_____, 19 ____.
(month and day)   (yr)

_____   _____
(Signature)   (Signature)

ORDER ADDITIONAL OR OTHER WORKBOOKS

WRITE YOUR OWN CONTRACTS OFFERS A TREMENDOUS VARIETY OF THE CONTRACTS MOST COMMONLY USED BY THE GENERAL PUBLIC TODAY WHENEVER TWO OR MORE PEOPLE WANT TO REACH AN AGREEMENT.

AND **SO** MUCH MORE!

PROMISSORY NOTES

BILLS OF SALE

POWER OF ATTORNEY

NOTICES

ARTICLES OF INCORPORATION

LIVING WILLS

ENCROACHMENT AGREEMENTS

LEASES

APPLICATIONS

WILLS

SUBLEASES

COUNTERPROPOSALS

FRANCHISE AGREEMENTS

INFORMATION FORMS

HOMESTEAD DECLARATIONS

AND EVEN MORE!

TAKE CHARGE AND SAVE MONEY!

PLACE STAMP HERE

WRITE YOUR OWN CONTRACTS
OGDEN SHEPARD PUBLISHING CO.
2305 CANYON BOULEVARD
BOULDER, CO   80302

ORDER ADDITIONAL OR OTHER WORKBOOKS

WRITE YOUR OWN CONTRACTS ORDER FORM

Each Workbook $14.95 Plus $1.50 Per Workbook for Postage/Handling

☐ Real Estate And Leases   ☐ Household / Landlord / Tenant $_____
                                                                  Amount for Book(s)
☐ Business   ☐ Family / Personal $_____
                                                                  Postage/Handling
                                                                  $_____
                                                                  Total Due

PRINT NAME _____

ADDRESS _____

CITY _____ STATE _____ ZIP _____

☐ PAYMENT ENCLOSED

CHECK APPROPRIATE BOX IF PAYING BY CREDIT CARD   ☐ AMEX   ☐ VISA   ☐ MASTERCARD

CREDIT CARD NUMBER _____ EXPIRATION DATE _____

SIGNATURE _____

ORDER ADDITIONAL OR OTHER WORKBOOKS

WRITE YOUR OWN CONTRACTS OFFERS A TREMENDOUS VARIETY OF THE CONTRACTS MOST COMMONLY USED BY THE GENERAL PUBLIC TODAY WHENEVER TWO OR MORE PEOPLE WANT TO REACH AN AGREEMENT.

ORDER ADDITIONAL OR OTHER WORKBOOKS

WRITE YOUR OWN CONTRACTS ORDER FORM

Each Workbook $14.95 Plus $1.50 Per Workbook for Postage/Handling

☐ Real Estate And Leases   ☐ Household / Landlord / Tenant

☐ Business   ☐ Family / Personal

$_____ Amount for Book(s)

$_____ Postage/Handling

$_____ Total Due

PRINT NAME _____

ADDRESS _____

CITY _____ STATE _____ ZIP _____

☐ PAYMENT ENCLOSED

CHECK APPROPRIATE BOX IF PAYING BY CREDIT CARD   ☐ AMEX   ☐ VISA   ☐ MASTERCARD

CREDIT CARD NUMBER _____ EXPIRATION DATE _____

SIGNATURE _____

ORDER NOW!

TAKE CHARGE AND SAVE MONEY!

PLACE
STAMP
HERE

WRITE YOUR OWN CONTRACTS
OGDEN SHEPARD PUBLISHING CO.
2305 CANYON BOULEVARD
BOULDER, CO 80302

CONTRACTS

APPLICATIONS

AGREEMENTS

BILLS OF SALE

NOTICES AND NOTES

AND

MUCH, MUCH MORE!